Jane Austen, or The Secret of Style

Jane Austen, or The Secret of Style

D. A. MILLER

PRINCETON UNIVERSITY PRESS

Princeton and Oxford

Published by Princeton University Press, 41 William Street,
Princeton, New Jersey 08540
In the United Kingdom: Princeton University Press,
3 Market Place, Woodstock, Oxfordshire OX20 1SY

LIBRARY OF CONGRESS CATALOGING-IN-PUBLICATION DATA
Miller, D. A., 1948–
Jane Austen, or The secret of style / D. A. Miller.
p. cm.
Includes bibliographical references (p.).
ISBN 0-691-09075-0 (alk. paper)
1. Austen, Jane, 1775–1817—Criticism and interpretation.
2. Women and literature—England—History—19th century.
3. Love stories, English—History and criticism. 4. Man-woman
relationships in literature. 5. Mate selection in literature.
6. Single women in literature. 7. Young women in literature.
8. Courtship in literature. 9. Marriage in literature.
I. Title: Jane Austen. II. Title: Secret of style. III. Title.
PR4037.M55 2003
813'.7–dc21   2002193067

British Library Cataloging-in-Publication Data is available

This book has been composed in Minion

Printed on acid-free paper. ∞

www.pupress.princeton.edu

Printed in the United States of America

10 9 8 7 6 5 4 3 2 1

I have no other resource but this *irony*:

to speak of the "nothing to say."

ROLAND BARTHES

Contents

Jane Austen, or The Secret of Style

ONE   Secret Love

I

All of us who read Jane Austen early—say, at eleven or twelve, the age when she began writing—were lost to the siren lure of her voice. "How nicely you talk; I love to hear you. You understand every thing."[1] Yet whereas Emma's talk merely held Harriet with the charm of a *person*, what Austen's writing channeled for us was the considerably more exciting appeal of no longer being one. Here was a truly out-of-body voice, so stirringly free of what it abhorred as "particularity" or "singularity" that it seemed to come from no enunciator at all. It scanted person even in the linguistic sense, rarely acknowledging, by saying *I*, its origination in an authoring self, or, by saying *you*, its reception by any other. We rapt, admiring readers might feel we were only eavesdropping on delightful productions intended for nobody in particular. And in the other constituents of person—not just body, but psyche, history, social position—the voice was also deficient, so much so that its overall impersonality determined a narrative authority and a beauty of expression both without equal. The former, bare of personal specifications that might situate and hence subvert it, rose to absoluteness; while the latter, likewise emptied of self, achieved classic self-containment. No extraneous static encumbered the dictation of a grammar that completed, and an art that finished, every crystalline sentence. Altogether, such thrillingly inhuman utterance was not stylish; it was Style itself.[2] In other words—the words of every lover at first sight—it was the thing that (our youth notwithstanding) *we had been waiting for all our lives.* From that singularity which, as Lady Russell knew, "makes the worst part of our suffering" (P 12), hadn't we longed for the same exemption? Let dull, docile Harriet be always content to "love to hear" Emma; in the boldness of our precocity, we were henceforward resolved to *speak* Austen Style, and to write it too. In the meantime, until we should acquire it, we indulged the fantasy of having done so. With the creative eye of daydream, we saw ourselves already wielding, already flashing the wondrous brand: saw its brilliant surface dazzle our enemies, and its sharp point, when they persisted in attack, pierce them to the quick; saw, to crown everything, its genius for detachment—for clean cuts—sever us once and forever from all the particulars of who and what we were, including of course those most responsible for the pain of our being thought peculiar.

Yet sooner or later, this experience of reading Jane Austen found itself contradicted—felt itself disabled—by the quite different experience of *being read* reading her. If the one moment, private and elective, united us all in common ecstasy, the other, public and compulsory, brought alienation into our midst, the mutual alienation of "girls" and "boys." For eventually— whether the "event" followed on our raptures, or occurred even before they had commenced (with trauma, who can be certain of sequence?)—popular opinion let us know that what should have sundered us from all identifying labels had in fact glued onto us one in particular: in short, that what we took for Style, everyone else took for Woman. Like a handbag or fragrance, the works of Jane Austen were deemed a "female thing"; and just as they were considered to bespeak the most distinctive depths of womanly being, so they were equally regarded as unreadable by those out of their natural element there. How could our reading not have noticed, not have suspected, so obvious and universally stamped a fact? Or, if informed by this fact, how could our reading have so far forgotten it as to sustain the very different fantasy of unconditioned being? Make no mistake: the girl reader as well as the boy had to negotiate the contradiction between the ghostly No One of enthralled imagination and the all-too-creaturely Woman of general consensus. But she at least had at her disposal some conspicuous sources of reconciliation. For one thing, what people said about Jane Austen could only enhance a girl's right relation to the sex system and to the culture it governed; she had done what a female not only would, but ought. Even better, by virtue of already anticipating, in her choice of books, the *grown-up* state of a female, she might think of herself as receiving precocity's most precious recognition, a certificate of adult-worthiness. But best of all, if Austen meant Woman, then perhaps in turn Woman might mean Austen, and a girl's command of the language of the one—a dialect, apparently, of her native tongue—would increase as her body continued developing the mature form of the other.

But the same discovery that, sometimes even despite herself, made the girl a good girl, made the boy all wrong. Plied with a Style whose unknown strength went straight to his head, he had fancied himself conquering the world with his swank Excalibur; now he woke to sobering sounds of derision and found that, during his intoxication, just as Lydia Bennet had done to another would-be soldier in *Pride and Prejudice*, Jane Austen had put him in a dress.[3] And upon the asinine transvestite spectacle he had been made to make of himself, one of two fates seemed necessarily to follow. Either he would no more be able to grow into Austen Style than into the Woman in whose name and nature the received idea had rooted it; or, on the contrary, in some less literal way, he might indeed grow into her, all the more easily in that apparently he had already begun doing so. But the completed process, if his present shamed state were any indication, would spell the most awful social doom imaginable. (When Mr. Knightley pronounces Frank Churchill's script "like a woman's writing," even the women he is addressing, Emma and Mrs. Weston, leap to vindicate it against what they consider a "base aspersion" [E 297].) In spite of her being, then, as Henry James famously put it, "one of those of the shelved and safe," Jane Austen had got the boy into trouble, and it was trouble that augured worse to come. Albeit her works regulated erotic desire so well that the world had judged them sexless, and made their author's very name a byword for chastity, they wound up giving their puerile reader, still at an age of sexual inexperience and vagueness, as much credit for an inclination to sex perversion as if they had been the wrong kind of pornography.

As Proust is always reminding us, though, we will do pretty much anything not to have to give up a pleasure; if occasionally the boy may have aborted his Austenophilia in repression, far more frequently he went on to indulge it in secret. "Let no name ever pass our lips. We were very wrong before; we will be cautious now" (342). Of his enduring attachment, then, consider this later example, in which, the general prophecy having come to pass, he is finally *practicing* his perversion.

> The butch number swaggering into a bar in a leather get-up opens his mouth and sounds like a pansy, takes you home, where the first thing you notice is the complete works of Jane Austen, gets you into bed, and—well, you know the rest.

This is Leo Bersani, ferociously ventriloquizing what he calls "the classic put-down" by gay men of one another's pretensions to manhood.[4] Even to its own sense of itself, the joke couldn't be more banal. Yet could it ever be too "tired," as we say, to *work*, to elicit automatically, from virtually any audience, the knowing laugh of folkloric literacy? On the contrary, the synergy of stereotypes motors an irresistible farce in which no sooner has the Woman been announced in the drawing room than, with duly inopportune eagerness, the Woman Inside charges out of the closet to rejoin her. And so continues into sexual maturity, even by his own kind, the shaming of the boy Austen reader, who seems (if we might keep up the shaming a bit longer) to have learned so little from past experience, to have amassed so meager a store of pop culture capital, that his childhood indiscretion is likely to go on being repeated till the end of his clueless days. As compulsively as the author of a "perfect crime" is undone by his unconscious need to get its perfection recognized, this incurable queen can't help laying his closet open to the view it was built to obstruct.

But the joke depends equally on a second recourse to Jane Austen, as secret as the first was open, and presupposing, besides the instant turnoff produced by her name, the thing perhaps least compatible with that reflex: a long and intimate acquaintance with her works. As anyone who dares boast a similar acquaintance may observe, this hidden Jane Austen ordains—both at large and, she would say, "at small" (L 163)— the very structure and tone of the joke. No doubt, this trick anecdote is as far from a marriage plot as the language in which it is related is free of the lexical and grammatical archaisms that signify Jane Austen in, for example, those misguided modern continuations of the novels where someone "is come" and something "put by." Precisely in the absence of these conventional signs of her, however, she is allowed to determine virtually everything else in the joke, from the confident ironic presentation of a universally acknowledged truth, to the wit that hones this truth into trenchant epigrammatic point, to the even more terrible sophistication that, while leaving its ostensible victim unaware of how he is being judged, keeps the dark cloud of shame that fails to descend on *him* hanging ominously over *us*, as our own prospective downfall if we should fail, or fail to pretend, to "know the rest."[5] Even a more literal kind of paper trail lies directly at hand in the precision of imitation that betrays, under the semblance of coarse sexual candor, the prim rhetoric employed by Miss Elizabeth Bennet with Darcy in *Pride and Prejudice*:

> My youngest sister has left all her friends—has eloped;—has thrown herself into the power of—of Mr. Wickham. They are gone off together from Brighton. *You* know him too well to doubt the rest. (PP 277)

But most of all, we recognize Austen in that *frozen* speech which at the moment of reaching us (as Roland Barthes once said of myth) "suspends itself, turns away and assumes the look of a generality."[6]

Ultimately, then, the joke allows us to distinguish two male readers of Jane Austen, a foolish and a clever. The foolish one has evidently fantasized "being" Jane Austen—being the woman she was—but ends up only being the object of ridicule in a quasi-Austenian comedy; while the clever one, more intelligently bent on "performing" Austen—on writing that comedy—mocks, scorns, disowns the very name of Jane Austen, and so contrives, anonymously and in secret, to carry on her work. He has transcended the status of a character whose slips are by definition always showing, by arrogating that of a narrator who, also by definition, makes use of those slips to confer volume and outline on the fictive person whom, ubiquitous and incorporeal, he can no longer resemble. For as he has understood it, Austen's work most fundamentally consists in *de-*

materializing the voice that speaks it. From the very start, his "I" has been commuted into a generalized "you"; and as for his voice, which in writing itself up as Austen Style, has lost its telltale vocal accents, who will ever be able to decide whether it sounds like a pansy's or not? This so-called narrator has in fact faded into that universal utterance which, even in Austen's own works, we can never quite read as *hers*; hence, in its appropriation here, isn't quite *his* either. Indeed, this fading somehow shifts our sexual understanding of him; from his role in the anecdote as a disappointed bottom, his accession to narration virtually refigures him into the voice of a supercilious top showing what Proust called "the contempt of the least homosexual for the most homosexual"[7]—and even into the general voice of heterosexuality itself, mocking the faggotry it observes from the unassailable distance of a spectator. And so, the contumely that the foolish queen draws on himself *for* reading Austen, that is, for being Woman, the clever one escapes *through* reading Austen, through having taken, practically as well as intellectually, the point of (her) Style.

But why do we speak of an escape, when such distinct traces allow us to catch the aspiring escape artist in the act, an act that thus would seem—along with the artist—manqué? Why do we call him clever, and not careless, when we may see, not far beneath his depersonalized, defeminized irony, his personal rage at having to forego the "female" sexual position; when we may show how his hard-hearted prose is as much—and ultimately, as transparent—a disguise as any leather getup; when, in sum, we possess all the wherewithal to do to this clever one just what he has done to his foolish other? It would be premature to answer these questions, which touch on what might be thought of as the *secret* of Style, before the extent of their bearing has been better grasped. I have so far presented the feminizing shame of Style (a shame that Style at once incurs and inflicts) as a very *narrowly* distributed abjection, peculiar to the minuscule band of juvenile Austen readers by whom it is first sustained, or to the closed company of the gay subculture in which it is post-traumatically confessed and mimed. A vulgar psychological reading might even find it most relevantly peculiar to myself, whose interest in Austen and the question of (her) Style would be reducible to this "personal" history. One way or another, in short, this question must seem circumscribed within the already vehemently circumscribed social category of the male homosexual; it is his "thing," or not even that: his thingy.

Yet the homosexual is never just himself, never constituted merely by his own aberrant desires and delights. A peripheral being, he nonetheless discharges a central function: that of a depository where certain disturbing experiences, desires, fantasies of the culture at large are placed for safe keeping, at once acknowledged and confined. The homosexual's "classic" pursuit of style is, among other things, his heroic way of rising to meet the fate projected on him in any case by a culture fearful of the extreme, exclusive, emptying, ecstatic character of *any* serious experience of Style. Whether in literature or film, few of modern narrative's master stylists—or *stylothetes*, as we do better to call them, for positing Style as the first principle, the a priori of their work—have failed to mount just this kind of lightning rod. From Wilde's too-pretty Dorian Gray, to Hitchcock's anal murderers with their "neat little touches," to Fellini's affected fairies—the logical fulfillment of a *dolce vita* in which, sooner or later, "we will all be homosexuals"—examples abound of a homosexual or analogously queered figure meant to draw off the charges of excess and aberrance from the excessive and aberrant oeuvre under construction. And against the tendency to regard such anxious, ambiguous scapegoating as an exclusively male practice, recall this fierce sarcasm from a woman not widely known for homophobia but famous for a style of her own. "Anyone who has the temerity to write about Jane Austen," an evidently brash Virginia Woolf wrote at the outset of an essay on that same subject, "is aware . . . that there are twenty-five elderly gentlemen living in the neighborhood of London who resent any slight upon her genius as if it were an insult to the chastity of their Aunts."[8] Already, in 1923, Austen Style needs to be acquitted of the peculiarities of a maiden aunt; and already, the means of acquittal is to pitch them, like some scalding hot potato, at the male aunties who love her for them. But of this maneuver, there is an even better, more pertinent example than Woolf's (which is complex enough, as she is implicitly arguing the case not just for Austen, but also, against Austen, for her own fiction). The whole elaborate and rather brutal game I have been describing, in which Austen Style may be collapsed into Woman and Woman into (male) Homosexual—or in which Austen Style, so as *not* to be collapsed into Woman, is collapsed into Homosexual directly—is not just played "around" Jane Austen. With equal ferocity and unrivaled skill, it has been played, first and foremost, "in" Jane Austen, as the shadow boxing of the great stylothete against herself. By way of once more affirming the deep Austenophilia of the gay man who ridicules Austen, the better to achieve (her) anonymous, defeminized Style, we turn to a symmetrical episode in Austen's own work, where she ridicules what might almost be a gay man, for a similar reason.

II

The episode comes from *Sense and Sensibility*; Elinor Dashwood, accompanied by her sister Marianne, has gone on an errand to Gray's, the London jewelry shop.

On ascending the stairs, the Miss Dashwoods found so many people before them in the room, that there was not a person at liberty to attend to their orders; and they were obliged to wait. All that could be done was, to sit down at that end of the counter which seemed to promise the quickest succession; one gentleman only was standing there, and it is probable that Elinor was not without hopes of exciting his politeness to a quicker dispatch. But the correctness of his eye, and the delicacy of his taste, proved to be beyond his politeness. He was giving orders for a toothpick-case for himself, and till its size, shape, and ornaments were determined, all of which, after examining and debating for a quarter of an hour over every toothpick-case in the shop, were finally arranged by his own inventive fancy, he had no leisure to bestow any other attention on the two ladies, than what was comprised in three or four very broad stares; a kind of notice which served to imprint on Elinor the remembrance of a person and face, of strong, natural, sterling insignificance, though adorned in the first style of fashion.

Marianne was spared from the troublesome feelings of contempt and resentment, on this impertinent examination of their features, and on the puppyism of his manner in deciding on all the different horrors of the different toothpick-cases presented to his inspection, by remaining unconscious of it all; for she was as well able to collect her thoughts within herself, and be ignorant of what was passing around her, in Mr. Gray's shop, as in her own bed-room.

At last the affair was decided. The ivory, the gold, and the pearls, all received their appointment, and the gentleman having named the last day on which his existence could be continued without the possession of the toothpick-case, drew on his gloves with leisurely care, and bestowing another glance on the Miss Dashwoods, but such a one as seemed rather to demand than express admiration, walked off with an happy air of real conceit and affected indifference.

    Elinor lost no time in bringing her business forward. . . . (SS 220–21)

Now, to put it mildly, there is nothing rare about jewelry in Jane Austen: not its value, not its beauty, and certainly not its distribution. If the first is too little interesting even to be assigned a price, the second is too little *dis*interesting ever to prompt appreciation "for its own sake." As for the third, it is so very wide that, if we could even imagine an Austen character with no right to exhibit a ring, earring, broach, bracelet, necklace, chain, cross, seal, miniature, or any of the other ornaments and trinkets that flood the represented social field, this unfortunate would be suffering as radical a deprivation as our own bourgeoisie fears for children whose parents haven't videotaped them. Still, the jewelry that circulates thus ubiquitously only does so under two quite limited conditions: it must always have been *given* to the wearer, and given *only* by a relative or lover, in token of union through marriage or common blood. (Friendship alone may neither bestow nor be signified by this gift; when Mary Crawford offers Fanny Price a necklace, its actual giver is Henry, who gave it to his sister in the first place, and now has asked her to pass it on to the woman he is courting.) No jewelry without donation, and no donation outside the prospect of alliance: that is the law governing the *bon usage* of jewelry in Austen. Solely under such regulation may it perform its proper, semiotic function, which is to signify not just alliance, but also the deeper (and sometimes warmer) attachment to the institutions exemplified in alliance: family and marriage. The reason that jewelry is not rare in Austen is simply that it cannot afford to be: it is the sign—and even some part of the substance—of everyone's required socialization.

Implicitly, of course, family and marriage complete one another, as Fanny recognizes when she joins William's cross and Edmund's chain, "those dearest tokens so formed for each other by every thing real and imaginary" (MP 271). But Austen's oeuvre, busy rehearsing conjugality's compulsions with a compulsiveness all its own, can hardly take equal interest in both tokens. As though yielding to *force majeure*, even kinship jewelry—Henry's brotherly gift of a necklace, or Edmund's cousinly one of a chain—gravitates toward circumnuptial resignification. The preeminent sign among all such signs, then, is the jewelry worn upon marriage itself: the wedding ring that Lydia Wickham fairly chafes to exhibit; the heirlooms that Frank Churchill is no less exultant in having new-set for Jane Fairfax; the ornaments paraded by Mrs. Elton because "a bride, you know, must appear like a bride" (E 302). The psychosocial investments in this jewelry are frankly exorbitant, but as such they merely match the exorbitant psychosocial investments in the married state, which counts, in Frances Ferguson's apt words, "as a breaking of the bank."⁹ The brightest gem never outshines the imagined splendor of the "establishment" that it signifies, or the institution whose discursive insistence overshadows Austen's entire world. Even when wedding jewelry occasions a display of vanity, this is only the craven vanity of successful socialization. As emblems of self-effacement, Mrs. Elton's elegant pearls and Isabella Thorpe's brilliant hoop rings quite hold their own against sackcloth and ashes; by flourishing the token of marriage, a woman becomes that token herself, a bride who truly does appear like a bride—and nothing but.

Who, then, in the scene before us, can fail to identify the trouble with that *bijou indiscret* which is the toothpick case, blatantly outside donation, alliance, social function, and signification? Even, say, a snuff box, though no less alienated from the major socializations of family and marriage, would remain the coffer from which tribute is paid to an ideal of (male) sociability: whatever is suspect about its intrinsic sheen is cleared by the homosocial epoxy accreted in its circulation. But unlike the snuff box, the toothpick case boasts the extreme "personal" character of its use, and—what comes to the same thing here, thanks to the ruthless perfectionism of the social superego that is providing our vantage point—the supreme inconsequence. Arguably, this chryselephantine bagatelle isn't a sufficiently social object even to convey such a boast—of those who will behold it at table with its owner, how many will have inclination, much less opportunity, to bestow on it the minute inspection that alone can do justice to its elegant, pointless intricacy? Certainly, none will ever share with him the single toothpick, of ivory or gold, that will be placed inside it. And how much does even this eventual placement matter? Empty, the case would seem just as splendid; and full, perhaps as futile—empty in effect. Yet this paltry content—the little bit of ivory that is the toothpick—is precisely what intensifies our sense that the container contains *nothing*. Just as the single, simple chair in the corner of an otherwise empty room is not placed there to fill the emptiness so much as to make the emptiness "full" (palpable, pervasive), so the puny toothpick that would pry open the case's closure to a purpose, that would penetrate and occupy its no longer hollow inner cavity, by performing these tasks ill, by exemplifying what we should call, in analogy with "bad form," *bad content*, only brings out the insistence of a self-containment where what is contained amounts to little more— to no more than a little more—than the container.

What is observable of the toothpick case, of course, is observable of the anonymous gentleman—later identified as Robert Ferrars, Edward's brother—who seems to have modeled his

future bauble on the strange bubble, impenetrable on the outside, but vacant within, that is all he presents of a self. (In
this regard, Austen contrasts him with Marianne, who, though
equally oblivious to what is passing around her, is nevertheless
able "to collect her thoughts within herself"; and, a fortiori,
with Elinor, whose unfailing good manners constrain her to
bury more deeply, hence allow her to cultivate more passion-
ately, the whole *croce e delizia* of nineteenth-century interiority.) Like his toothpick case in another respect too, however,
Robert is not quite so indifferent, or so vacuous, as he would
appear; somewhere inside him he harbors, if not a toothpick,
some other little prick busy throwing the indifference and the
vacuity into aggressive high relief. Elinor is furious that he pays
her no consideration because he does pay her enough to rub
her nose in the fact; and he galls her with a vacancy that is
evidently not devoid of the will to display itself, to make her
take it in as, hatefully, her own. In a world that is nothing if not
consistently intelligible, and where the main work of making it
so is given over to "person and face," to the expressive air, ad-
dress, and manners of the one, and to the meaningful looks,
winks, glows, blushes, smiles, smirks, sneers, or sighs of the
other, "insignificance" in both may be the gravest charge Elinor
knows how to articulate; and assuredly, under its force, the
human toothpick case comes to embody, beyond an individual
shallowness of socialization and subjectivity, the danger of their
general flattening, even undoing.

Plainly, though, a chief cause of Elinor's animus is the insignificance with which Robert afflicts one thing in particular:
male heterosexuality. Whether through mercenary motives or
dishonorable intentions, other men—those Franco Moretti has
called the "swindlers" of Austen's marriage market[10]—threaten
the marriage plot with an unhappy ending, but this man, a
more radical enemy to matrimony, would prevent it from ever

getting started. Beyond "politeness," beyond, that is, the male gallantry that dutifully fashions every encounter with "the sex" into the miniature of a *courtship*, he seems equally remote from the erotic interest in women that is courtship's prerequisite. His inspection clearly does not offer Elinor what Anne Elliot is so gratified to receive from that of a passing stranger in *Persuasion*: the proof, "by the gentleman's looks, that he thought hers very lovely" (P 104). It is not Elinor's to-be-looked-at-ness, or Marianne's, that Robert's broad stares are meant to establish, but his own; in examining their features, he would only be assessing the competition for visual attention. And if his fetishistic to-do over a mere toothpick, which no amount of compensatory packaging will ever render less piddling, hints perhaps that he *can't* perform with a woman, the complete pick-and-case set raises the much more unsettling possibility that, like a self-fertilizing flower, he *doesn't need to*: no sexual lack in himself would impel him to one for its satisfaction. In sum, we should sooner confuse the toothpick case with a wedding band than take the gemlike flame who personifies it for the marrying kind.

When in the end Robert does marry, this is the novelist's intended surprise, as carefully sprung as the unforeseen solution of a mystery writer who observes the rule of the least likely suspect. We learn that Elinor's rival, Lucy, has finally managed to become "Mrs. Ferrars"; only Mrs. Ferrars proves to be not Mrs. *Edward* Ferrars, as both Elinor and the reader fear, but Mrs. *Robert* Ferrars, which, thanks to this cleverly misleading scene, no one could have imagined. Its elegant solution, however, does little to make the riddle less of a mystery. The psychological problem of Robert's motivation is hardly successfully finessed by being passed off as the solution to a structural puzzle about the identity of "Mrs. Ferrars." Elinor considers the match "one of the most extraordinary and unaccountable circumstances she has ever heard," quite "beyond her comprehension to make out"; and it excites "unceasing and reasonable wonder" in everyone else too (SS 364). Even after an explanation is offered, in which most of Robert's motivation is elided into the more easily given account of Lucy's, and the rush to closure excuses the lameness of the part that is necessarily left perfunctory, Robert's share in the event remains no less completely a puzzle than Elinor first thought it, as though the author's wish to correct Robert's unheterosexual attitude were too urgent to be routed through her usual verisimilitude.

"Unheterosexual" I've called this attitude, for we can't safely be more precise about it than that. If we imagined the first phase in some unwritten Hegelian history of sexuality, where heterosexual being has called forth its own not-being, but the latter has not yet synthesized any positive content of its own, Robert would represent that phase, a shadow of sexual dissidence that has no substance but a refusal, the norm denied. He is what Wilde later dreamed, but fell short, of being: a sphinx without a specifiable secret. No doubt, this sphinx insinuates the themes of hermaphroditism and inversion that would have so spectacular a discursive future later in the century, and which were already, in Austen's own day and culture, coming to acquire a certain typological consistency. Already, too, as a later chapter informs us, an all-powerful, doting mother—"Robert always was her favourite" (366)—presides over the incipient iconography, to model his effeminate "puppyism," and to mirror his narcissistic "conceit." But because Austen's historical moment precedes the epistemological conquest of "the homosexual" by over a half-century; because her social position as a "lady" obliges her to seem ignorant of certain matters, if it does not actually keep her so; and perhaps even because, characterologically, the labor of constructing a closet leaves Robert no leisure for committing the indecencies to be shut in there, all these intimations remain barren. Wilde's ambition to be all enigmatic, teasing form was eventually betrayed by the hidden truth that inspired it, and whose public disclosure—as an aberrant, abhorrent, but nonetheless replete psychosexual *identity*—reduced that form to its thoroughly broken code. By contrast, the integral portrait of Robert confirms the utter un-representability of anything beyond the signs that, in anticipa-tion of their social failure to signify, have already become signs of insignificance. Another instance of "bad content," his little bit of proto-homosexuality merely shades an all the more purely felt blankness. Austen's arbitrary refashioning of him at the end seems hardly more arbitrary than his own self-fashion-ing in the beginning, for he has refused heterosexuality on the grounds of what appears to be *almost nothing*.

On the grounds, to put it more positively, of a certain *style* ("the correctness of his eye," "the delicacy of his taste," "the first style of fashion"). For style here is not merely another general name, like insignificance, for the particular insuffi-ciencies of substance—the want of civility, of inwardness, of hetero-hymeneal meaning—that we have seen characterize the toothpick case and its personification in Robert. Unlike insig-nificance, which denotes a condition, style presupposes a delib-erately embraced project. Insignificance might only befall one; whereas style, as the activist *materialization* of insignificance, one must choose, pursue, perform. "All style and no sub-stance": the formula helps us recognize not that style is *differ-ent*, or even *opposite*, to substance (and hence capable of being united with it, as Mr. Elliot ostensibly supports "the solid" with "the superficial" in *Persuasion* [P 146]), but that the one is in-compatible with, and even corrosive of the other. Style can only emerge at the expense of substance, as though it sucked up the latter into the vacuum swollen only with the "airs" it gives itself. It is thanks to style that Robert, more than just a hapless casu-alty of semiotic blight, is felt by Elinor to be the actual agent from whom, through his blank, staring eyes, it emanates. (When he is said to convey insignificance "*though* adorned in the first style of fashion," the text of course means us to substitute: *because.*) And in Elinor's dysphoric experience of it, his will to style also makes us experience the willfulness of that will. If insignificance has nothing to say for itself, style, also having nothing to say, insists on our hearing it all the same. The irritating paradox of Robert's marked style is that, even as she dismisses this style as having no substance, Elinor nonetheless feels it to *be in the way.* For all its ostensible nothingness, it condenses, and displays, an exasperating materiality that won't disappear into social meaning, or even simply—so exigent is the demand for such meaning—disappear *quickly enough.* Worse than Robert's fussing in Elinor's eyes is the dilatoriness of that fussing. From the excessive length of time he consumes first in looking for, then in designing, a toothpick case, through the rallentando of his looks-become-stares, to, finally, the "leisurely care" with which he puts on his gloves before departing, his is a waste that refuses to make haste. Much as, at Gray's today, the attention-riveting beep of a cell phone announces a second, more deafening aggression to come, the prattle that is jammed into our ears when the call is taken, so Robert's stylistic "excess" is nothing next to the far more harassing ostentation of itself that Elinor is obliged to witness.

In other words, what is socially deviant in Robert's foppishness—the unheterosexual effeminacy that shrinks the bachelor pool—is less infuriating than what, despite this aberrance, remains normal. All of Austen's other pokey shoppers are female; think of Harriet Smith, who, "tempted by every thing and swayed by half a word, was always very long at a purchase" (E 233), or of Robert's own fellow character in this novel, Charlotte Palmer, "whose eye was caught by every thing pretty, expensive, or new; who was wild to buy all, could determine on none, and dawdled away her time in rapture and indecision" (SS 165). The difference is crying: Robert does the same silly-feminine thing as Miss Smith and Mrs. Palmer—spending an inordinate amount of time on a trifle—but he does it with the cool, easy, altogether undisputed authority of a man who assumes—and imposes on all around him—the full importance of this silly-feminine thing. For all that Robert reveals the Woman in him, her blatant presence fails to rob him of the smallest bit of male entitlement. Elinor may be outraged by his assurance, but, of the many middle-class men and women with whom we find him associating, no one else takes the slightest exception to it; indeed, to Elinor's own brother, John, "there can be no difference" between Robert and Edward: "they are both very agreeable young men, I do not know that one is superior to the other" (297). Astonishingly, Robert *gets away with it*: he manages to perform the feminine thing without suffering a concomitant social demotion. Having entirely given up virility, the various behaviors that give masculinity its content, he has nonetheless retained the phallus that gives them their ideal form.

Much better than Austen's manly heroes, then, the effeminate Robert teaches us the immense power, and the inestimable value, of an authority so sure of itself, so always-already taken for granted, that it doesn't even need the naturalizing alibi of a virile mission. "Silly things do cease to be silly," thinks Emma apropos of Frank Churchill's haircut, "if they are done by sensible people in an impudent way" (E 212). Elinor seems to be making a related, but considerably more bitter discovery: that silly things cease to be silly simply by being done with all-sufficient, male authority. Mr. Knightley and Captain Wentworth, both of whom possess this authority, must also be thought of as "deserving" it, or at least as amply *paying* for it, the former through administrative leadership of Highbury, the latter through empire-building exploits on the high seas. What infuriates—what fascinates—in the effeminate man is not his femininity, but the maleness that insists on surviving it. What Austen calls "the ostentation of a coxcomb" (212) is precisely this spectacle of an authority so magisterial that even devirilization cannot lessen it. And this is also what, finally, Robert is offering as his "style."

III

"Whatever its sophistication, style has always something crude about it." What Barthes seems to have in mind with this remark is the brute intimacy of style—as the "decorative voice of hidden, secret flesh"—with the body of its practitioner.[11] Certainly, much of what may be called crude about Robert's style depends on the fact that the occasion for stylistic elaboration, the stimulus to the "delicacy of taste"—in short, the toothpick—is not merely a trivial object, but also a vulgar one: an awkward, even somewhat embarrassing implement for removing and disposing of matter that, however originally tempting as "food" on the plate, has perhaps only minutes later, and with no digestion having taken place, become unappetizingly visible on or between the teeth as "waste." In this sense, the affront of style would have to do with a revolting decomposition which style's defiantly, pathetically compensatory *composure* never perfectly succeeds in sublimating, thus falling under the suspicion of not trying hard enough, perhaps not really trying at all.

But what interests me more about style in this scene is the crudeness of the attack on it, the strange fits of brutality that come over character and narrative voice alike in condemning it. When style is to be scourged in Austen, the rods must evidently be quite blunt, appealing to nothing finer than the common sense of "obvious" social notions. Elinor dismisses from her mental activity its usual companions—doubt, hesitation, puzzlement, curiosity, discrimination, ambivalence, reflection —so that her mere observation is already passing a summary judgment. And in presenting Robert's "first style," Austen too forgoes the subtle comedy for which she is famous, so as to write what is arguably the glibbest scene in her entire work. The trouble with Robert, his toothpick case, their shared "first style," this trouble *speaks for itself*, and speaks so unequivocally that the only wonder remaining—the only thing that is not obvious, and might pose a problem for everything that is—is how Robert himself has failed to notice such abundance of self-evidence.

This scandal—of an obvious social evil not even dimly perceived as such by its unabashed perpetrator—is what lends the censure of style its characteristic savagery, as though, to be fully protected against style, our bluntness of perception needed to acquire a second bluntness, that of an instrument of injury. Usually choosing to smile and be amused at the nonsense of her fellow creatures, here Elinor vents a "contempt and resentment" that only a uniquely violent affront—or a singularly dangerous appeal—could warrant. And only a technical, a formal distinction exists between her perceptions and the narration that thus shows no interest in ironizing them. Much as a reviewer, having torn a sentence out of its context in a book whose style he wishes to deride, confidently quotes it in full without comment—for the sentence (like a sissy whom a bully has yanked from his books, or deprived of his glasses) now looks unprotected enough to provoke, and stupid enough to deserve, our reliably forthcoming abuse—so, Austen seizes on the toothpick case as evidence that would go without saying, would conjoin us all with Elinor in the happy security of an interpretive community with nothing to interpret, and in an equally imaginary immunity from the effects of a style thus damningly established as the style of the Other.

Yet even a hack may be shown to be strangely drawn to the thing he loves to hate, or, not at all strangely, dependent on the thing he makes his name and his living by belittling: you will never catch him writing about the sober prose that he claims to be speaking for; it probably bores him, and certainly could never spur him to the opinionated vehemence with which he is asked to "make new" our continued submission to the most familiar social demands. But if even this hack may be caught in secret complicity, what are we to say of that founder of Style who is Jane Austen? of that Jane Austen who, though she is often cruel, seldom seems crude? The scene positively flushes with the clandestine intimacy of its link to what, in its sheer obviousness, it has been designed not to recognize. What is Elinor's *own* business at Gray's but to carry on "a negociation for the exchange of a few old-fashioned jewels of her mother" (SS 220)? No more than Robert is she there to traffic in trinkets of alliance; she is there simply to exchange what is "old-fashioned" for what is not. The dubious exigencies of "the first style" have brought her to Sackville Street too. Indeed, with the exception of Robert's case, Elinor's mother's jewels are the only ones in all of Austen's work whose chief purpose is not to recognize a relationship, nor to claim their bearer on behalf of sociality, but to signify a certain independent relation to *style*. And Elinor's mirroring of Robert in this respect carries over to every other, almost to the end of the scene. After all, she could hardly detect the broadness of his stares, or take the mnemonic imprint of his "insignificance," without some pretty direct and sustained looking of her own. Her corrective eye meets his correct one, no less mimetically than the insignificance ascribed to him by her anger matches the nullification worked on her by his hauteur; as he ignores her womanliness, so she disdains his manhood. And—what unites all these details—she assumes an attitude, affects a stony indifference that, much more certainly than he, she is far from actually feeling.

To give the matter its furthest consequence, let us observe that what always implicitly frames this scene at Gray's is a different kind of jewelry from the one that has so far concerned us: the kind that comes to mind when we think of language compacted into small-sized specimens of spectacular beauty and perfection; the jewelry, in other words, that provides the metaphor for epigram, for wit, for that cool, compressed adequation of language to whatever it wants to say which I will be calling Absolute Style. For all these things, our culture offers us only one other metaphor: the rapier and its punctual relations (the pin, the needle, the knife, the teeth). But when wit—to take a privileged version of Absolute Style—is not sharp, keen, cutting, or incisive, then it is brilliant, dazzling, crystalline, sparkling, glittering, coruscating, diamondlike, lapidary, precious; and its best specimens, if not called "hits" or "attacks," are spoken of as "gems" and "pearls." Unsurprisingly, for better and worse, the metaphor of jewel work has dominated the reception of Austen's work from the start, when Mary Russell Mitford observed that "till *Pride and Prejudice* showed what a precious gem was hidden in that unbending case, [Austen] was no more regarded in society than a poker,"[12] down to our own era, in which Lord David Cecil found it necessary to affirm, against those who thought Jane Austen was a mere "manufacturer of snuff-boxes," that she was not.[13] More pertinently, the jewel metaphor subtends the novelist's own account of verbal style in her characters. If Elizabeth Bennet is truly "the brightest jewel of the country" (PP 384), as Sir William Lucas calls her, it is because her complexion's "brilliancy" (33), epitomized in her eyes' "beautiful expression" (23), equally marks the well-formed expressions that fall from her mouth with "all the eclat of a proverb" (91). Miss Bingley's presumably lame "witticisms on [her rival's] *fine eyes*"(46) only help us to see how fully those eyes, in their gemlike brilliancy, authenticate Elizabeth's own superior practice of wit. And even Mrs. Elton, "as elegant as . . . pearls could make her" (E 292), "mean[s] to shine" (272) not just by means of the abundant bridal ornaments she sports, but also by her "sparkling vivacity" (457).

But most important, of course, is Austen's recourse to the jewel metaphor in both of the only two aesthetic pronouncements she ever made on her work, where we find the same ambivalence that characterizes the metaphor in her critical reception, and determines its distribution among her characters. In the first of these pronouncements, she professed to complain that *Pride and Prejudice* was "too light & bright & sparkling," where *light,* the crucial switchword, refers us equally to the admirable colorlessness of the jewel ("the less yellow the diamond") and to the contemptible symbolic and material weightlessness of the trinket (L 203). In the second pronouncement, still more famous, she described her work as "the little bit of ivory (two inches wide) on which I work with so fine a Brush as produces little effect after much labor" (189). Now it is the ivory miniature that represents the "precious" both in bono and in malo; and though the delicacy of the brush does not exempt it from intense labor, the productivity of such labor is slight, even doubtful, as though the artist were deliberately taking the greatest pains to produce a thing that must be as futile as it aspires to be fine.

Austen arrives at Gray's, then, by a twofold route. As a literal place where the accessories signifying licensed affections are made, chosen, sold, and whose very name repeats that of the Miss Grey whom Willoughby has just married, the jewelry shop is an obvious thematic way station in the marriage plot. Here, where the norms of that plot are everywhere felt, it is perfectly natural that Elinor, an unmarried woman suffering the ruin of her own conjugal prospects, as well as her sister's, should be so quick to register and resent any apparent male deviations; and that Austen, serving the marriage plot as its aging maid of honor, should be so spiteful in "correcting" these (to the point of marrying Robert off to someone that he himself has described as "the merest awkward country girl, without style, or elegance, and almost without beauty" [SS 299]). But as the figurative manufactory of the brilliant, the sparkling, the precious, the lapidary, the engraved—where, among the miniatures, we might find that miniature of miniatures that is "the little bit of ivory"—the jewelry shop must also be the equally natural *mise-en-abîme* of Austen Style, its implicit home and place of self-meditation. Simultaneously determined by narrative thematics and the course of stylistic reflection, the shop situates a collision between the claims of the literal gem, which, as a properly functional item, must never degenerate into idle refinement, as it does with Robert, and those of the figurative gem, an eminently aesthetic thing whose social destination is vague, mysterious, trifling, troublesome. And this collision in turn figures the tension, everywhere visible in Austen, between her typical subject (the marriage plot that excludes the author, a world in which the author's condition, as an author, can't be represented) and her characteristic voice (the exclusiveness of Absolute Style).[14] More to our point, though, the scene also stages a confrontation between two styles, between the one represented, Robert's, and the one representing it, Austen's, or No One's. I have said enough to suggest that No One's Style, in censuring Robert's, in giving it the ridiculousness that it deserves, is simultaneously free to borrow many of its central gestures, to realize in itself the fantasy of autarchy that, for Robert, it has just rendered impossible. Not only does Robert's style work a miracle, the miracle of the "female thing" performed with male authority, but also, like other miracles, it brings inspiration, and what it inspires is nothing less than that superior duplication of itself which is Austen Style.

At the macroscopic level of such duplication, notice how overelaborated the entire episode seems to be with regard to what needs to be known about Robert or his relative importance in the novel, how largely gratuitous it remains—a kind of narrative toothpick case itself, constructed largely for its own sake, with little care for novelistic functionality, until the very end, when a toothpick (the function of misleading us about Robert's marriageability) is finally put in it. Notice, too, at the microscopic level, how the first sentence that lifts the prose into any complexity, the first sentence to exceed mere reportage and strike the characteristic Austenian note, reproduces, in its own suddenly expansive syntax, Robert's own deferral in coming to any point:

> He was giving orders for a toothpick-case for himself, *and till its size, shape, and ornaments were determined, all of which, after examining and debating for a quarter of an hour over every toothpick-case in the shop, were finally arranged by his own inventive fancy,* he had no leisure to bestow any other attention on the two ladies, than what was comprised in three or four very broad stares. . . . [emphasis added]

It is as though the text were excited to its own production by this "attitude," this indifference, this freedom from ordinary social necessity which it calls style, but which it can only have by disowning it—by ridiculing, shaming, correcting it in someone or something else. The first secret of Austen Style: its author hates style, or at any rate, must always say she does; she must always profess the values, and uphold the norms, of "nature," even as she practices the most extraordinarily formal art the novel had yet known. (At Pemberley, "a stream of some natural importance was swelled into greater, but without any artificial appearance. Its banks were neither formal, nor falsely adorned" [PP 245]. The prose can be conspicuously formal because it conspicuously values a stream that is not.) But Robert's attitude, reproduced as the text, is not *simply* duplicated; it is duplicated within a structure that negates it. The general form of this structure in Austen is that anonymous, impersonal, universal narration (usually called, after its least important feature, omniscient) which can always catch Robert out in an embarrassing peculiarity from which it itself is, by its very status, free. And this general structure realizes itself most pointedly—and intimately—as free indirect style, in which the narration's way of *saying* is constantly both mimicking, and distancing itself from, the character's way of *seeing*.[15] Both forms are Austen's greatest and most recognized contributions to culture, but they are also her weirdest, and her least assimilable, and I will have more to say about them in the chapters to come. But for now, let me only observe that Robert's attitude, his male authority in doing the female thing, offers at once a rudimentary model for the achievement of Austen Style, and one that is far *too* rudimentary. An early burlesque by Thackeray, *The Tremendous Adventures of Major Gahagan*, begins with a pair of brothers, twinned down to their monograms, fighting a duel over a toothpick case that each claims as his own; but such specularity of enemy doubles is precisely what Austen Style would have already overcome here. For Austen Style is *not* Robert's style, or is Robert's style only after the latter has been closeted and chastened, and all its concrete flamboyance disciplined into the austere abstraction of structure.

By means of this eccentric scene, however, in which Austen, uncharacteristically allegorical, seems to open the secret of (her) Style, we learn that this abstraction is best understood as *the work of abstracting*—that it comes into being as a willed denial of particularities whose traces nonetheless persist in giving it, not its structure, which is what negates them, but something more intimate: its texture, that constant reminder of what remains unsublated. Nor is this a merely a case of Pierre Bourdieu's "distinction," in which style would secure class privilege in relation to the style-impaired vulgarity that it is always trumping. What lies at the close heart of Austen Style is much more particular: a failed, or refused, but in any case shameful relation to the conjugal imperative. Outside that imperative, Robert also stands outside the elaborate socialization that prepares and rewards us for our obedience to it, and this double exteriority is what renders him vacuous and inane, an almost self. His style would replace the self that, in any full historical, social, or (above all) novelistic way, can't yet cohere into something besides abjection. Behind the glory of style's willed evacuation of substance lies the ignominy of a subject's *hopelessly insufficient social realization,* just as behind style's ahistorical impersonality lies the historical impasse of someone whose social representation doubles for social humiliation. Granted, Robert is "all style"; but suppose he were not. Given Austen's world, could his unheterosexuality ever seize enough social fabric to fashion him into a "person" of substance? As I hope to show in the next chapter, Austen Style similarly presupposes, and enforces, its author's own "under-representability," a condition I can describe most simply for the moment by observing that the realism of her works allows no one like Jane Austen to appear in them. Amid the happy wives and pathetic old maids, there is no successfully unmarried woman; and despite the multitude of girls who seek to acquire "accomplishments," not one shows an artistic achievement or even an artistic ambition that surpasses mediocrity. The social grounding is insufficient, not of course for this woman to exist—she does, she is Jane

Austen—but to entitle her existence to the same dignity of novelistic representation that she gives Elizabeth and Emma, or even Mrs. Elton and Lady Bertram. Like the Unheterosexual, the Spinster too resorts to Style, the utopia of those with almost no place to go.

TWO   No One Is Alone

I

Of that godlike authority which we think of as the default mode
of narration in the traditional novel, Jane Austen may well be
the *only* English example. Whether our standard is Fielding in
the eighteenth century, or Thackeray in the nineteenth, the omniscient narrator's divinity proves constantly betrayed by his
human verisimilitude, the all-too-familiar "character" with
which he can't help tending to coincide. Pronounced with the
thick accent of the sociolect that immediately sits him down on
one or another chair of distinctly institutional, unmistakably
male authority, his omniscience seems hardly more than a poet-
ically licensed exaggeration of the kinds of empowered knowledge that are already possessed, already displayed and exercised,
by various men in the nonfictional world: a learned magistrate,
say, or a gossipy clubman. Far from enacting a fantasy of divine
authority, the noisy personalities of Fielding and Thackeray re-
lentlessly humanize that authority, never let us forget its earthly
origins as a glamorization of some garden-variety male know-
it-all. Even George Eliot, when not occupied with simulating
such a figure, ventriloquizes the well-remembered voice of that
all-knowing, all-understanding, and all-forgiving woman to

whom—uniquely—everyone has been accustomed to submit: the mother. These canonical examples of omniscient narration are only canonical in that they represent the Feuerbachian tendency everywhere present in it to bring the gods down to earth. By contrast, Austen's divinity is free of all accents that might identify it with a socially accredited broker of power/knowledge in the world under narration.[16] It does not carry on either from the authority of the commanding, intelligent, but hardly style-conscious hero, or from that of the elegant, witty heroine, with a mind "darkened, yet fancying itself light" (MP 367). However doubtful it must be that Jane Austen is a writer for all time—who could ever prove this?—she always writes like a real god, without anthropomorphism. Nowhere else in nineteenth-century English narration have the claims of the "person," its ideology, been more completely denied.

Hence, the staring paradox of Austen's narration: it is at once utterly exempt from the social necessities that govern the narrated world, and intimately acquainted with them down to their most subtle psychic effects on character. It does not itself experience what it nonetheless knows with all the authority of experience. For an early example, recall the moment in *Northanger Abbey* when Catherine Morland has got lost in the Tilneys' discussion of the picturesque:

> She was heartily ashamed of her ignorance. A misplaced shame. Where people wish to attach, they should always be ignorant. To come with a well-informed mind, is to come with an inability of administering to the vanity of others, which a sensible person would always wish to avoid. A woman especially, if she have the misfortune of knowing any thing, should conceal it as well as she can. (NA 110–11)

If we extend this truth (offered as a general one) to its enunciation, we can't but reach one of two conclusions. The first is, quite simply, that *this truth must be false.* Someone, the enunciator, *does* know something and, by no means attempting to conceal it, has publicly and rather proudly uttered it. Furthermore, contrary to the wounding effect that such outspoken knowledge is supposed to have on the vanity of others, this specimen of it wins us over no less than Catherine's shy ignorance conquers Henry. For of course, we do believe in this insight, and must; otherwise Austen would have "nothing to say," and the whole readerly transference of which we have made her authority the object would be placed in jeopardy. But if the first conclusion is inadmissible, then we are obliged to adopt the second: namely, that *the enunciator is not a woman*—not a woman, at any rate, in the defining social sense of the passage: one who wishes to "attach," who must get attached willy-nilly. The least revised of Austen's early novels, *Northanger Abbey* still intermittently features a personal narrator; but even here, where it has not yet attained the full purity of its impersonality, Austen Style is already decidedly *neuter*, as though it were on an exemption from "sex"—in the old-fashioned sense (appropriate for the epoch) of both gender *and* sexuality—that this impersonality is most crucially founded, developed, secured. (Analogously, only in her first published novel does Austen go by the pen name, already announcing the anonymity she took such care to preserve, of "a Lady": "*Sense and Sensibility*: A Novel; in three volumes; by a Lady." In subsequent works, she simply identifies herself as the author of the previous ones, and the Lady becomes increasingly difficult to retrieve: "*Pride and Prejudice*, by the Author of *Sense and Sensibility*"; "*Mansfield Park*, by the Author of *Sense and Sensibility* and *Pride and Prejudice*"; "*Emma*, by the Author of *Pride and Prejudice* &c. &c."[17])

Yet, as I've been showing, Austen's austere forms tend to abstract specific oppressions that continue, in varying degrees of faintness, to color them. The narrative voice here, like a slightly bungled sex-change operation that leaves a tiny reminder of the gender it has altered (say, Hedwig's "angry inch"), blows its neutrality, if only just a little bit, in the animus it betrays toward men who are weak enough to require, or credulous enough to believe, the assurance of female ignorance. Now, we know that the founding gesture of Austen Style is the cut (in testimony to which, every reader sooner or later resorts to calling it "precise," "concise," "incisive"). We also know that, however trenchantly this Style may deal with characters, its first object has been itself, manifestly the result of rigorous selection, exclusion, reduction. Even if its author hadn't told us, anyone might know of *Pride and Prejudice* that it had been "lopt & cropt" (L 202). But in Austen's mature work, the scar left by this cut is vague and indeterminate: we infer *that* excision has taken place, but are not allowed to specify just *what* has been excised. Whereas the somewhat naive narrator of *Northanger Abbey* effectively declares, "I am not Woman," "I do not submit to female social necessity," "I do not need to get married," the mature narration encourages us to think of it in truncated intransitives: "it is not," "it does not submit," "it does not need," period. The heady *promesse du bonheur* that the great first sentence of *Pride and Prejudice* extends to us, despite the fact that it too lends its authority to acknowledging the depressing law of universal conjugality, comes down to one thing: that no one who writes with such possession can be in want of *anything*. The sentence self-evidently issues from a state of already having achieved—or, at any rate, of having entirely dispensed with the need to achieve—everything that, for instance, the typical nineteenth-century ambition plot seeks to obtain, and even more. But the fact of enjoying, or imagining enjoying, the happy ending of a plot that one has been spared the labor of working through, makes the sentence merely a pleasant daydream. The fact of enjoying, or imagining enjoying, the happy ending of a plot that, except in this mode of writing, one never *could* perform—a plot that otherwise, even within its middle-class confines, one must know only as fore-closed—this is what makes the sentence the ecstatic and strangely wrenching experience it has always been. Even in its narrower stated terms, since the necessity of getting a spouse, though weighing on man too, is felt to weigh more heavily on woman, the exempted condition of being neither one acquires more female than male pertinence; and accordingly there hangs over the Austen Neuter the iconoclastic possibility that it may not be the Neuter at all, but only an exquisitely masked femi-nine desire for it.

More: if the Neuter must never acknowledge that it is *unat-tainable*, forever relapsing into the gender from which it would have worked free, neither must it admit that it is already *real-ized*, by those malformed social subjects who have been, for one reason or another, thrown out of sex. Into the wishfully reparative key of abstraction, the Neuter may have merely transposed the dismal condition of *the neutered*. Consider, for instance, the case of Roland Barthes, who first theorized the Neuter in the ultralinguistic sense of the term as I've been using it, that is, not to classify a substantive, but to incite a kind of writing practice that refuses the alternative of gender specifica-tion. In Barthes's rendition, the Neuter, by causing this alterna-tive to blur, gives entry to a Shangri-La of "delectable insignifi-cance," "the vacancy of 'the person,' " "the absence of *imago*," "discretion," "the principle of delicacy," and "a happy sexual-ity."[18] Yet throughout the Barthesian oeuvre, this Neuter is haunted by an uncannily repulsive resemblance to that famil-iarly given formulation of the homosexual as "neither man nor woman" which is so essential both to his real marginalization and to the fearsome fantasmatic grandeur called on to justify it. Could "discretion," for example, ever be discreet enough to finesse its well-known genealogy in shame and coercion? And though in his great late works, Barthes *performs* this Neuter with unmatched seductiveness, even he can only find it *repre-sented*—made social flesh—in the literally emasculated figure of the castrato in Balzac's "Sarrasine." Embodied by this (suffering, tragic, impossible) *creature*, as he is repeatedly called, what Barthes would transvalue as "vacancy of 'the person'" inspires only the dread of what Balzac more commonsensically abominates as "form without substance."[19]

Now recall, from elsewhere in Balzac, from *Père Goriot*, the sign over the Maison Vauquer: *pension bourgeoise des deux sexes et autres* ("middle-class boarding house for both sexes and others"), where the ostensibly fantastic category of "others" comes to be occupied not simply by Vautrin, the homosexual, but also by Mademoiselle Michonneau, the old maid. For the figure of the old maid stands in the same pertinence to Austen's practice of the Neuter as that of the homosexual does to Barthes's: the sad figure who is the sole personification of the Neuter "in the world." It is, after all, the old maid's regular destiny—contradicted by nothing in all Austen, including all Austen—to fall out of sex in every sense but an anatomical one. Even before contrariousness puts its mark on her temperament, contradiction has already determined her social place. What Elinor, for instance, fears in Robert's uncomplaisant stare is not *his* perversity, so much as the perversity to which it seems to destine *her*: the counterfinality of a state in which her ineradicable socialization would be obliging her, always and everywhere, to acknowledge a meaningfulness that condemns her to insignificance. No doubt good Miss Bates, also known as poor Miss Bates, wins herself some small place of regard by endlessly thanking society for its tolerance (albeit granted in the *irritated* forms of avoidance and ridicule) toward the conjugally irrelevant. She must bear nonetheless the same unsexed appellation as Balzac's castrato. She is "a good creature," "there is not a better creature in the world," she "thought herself a most fortunate creature" (E 286, 375, 21); but she is not a woman in any sense that is interesting either to society or to a novel whose own achievement of social centrality depends on her marginalization.[20]

Far from doing much to alter this state of affairs, Austen refines it into unexceptional consistency. The recorder of Emma's ample inner life categorically refuses to Miss Bates any of the reserve that is its precondition, just as in Diana Parker's lively imagination, the painstaking artist finds only the inventiveness of hypochondria, and in her "restless activity," only busywork. The unendurable garrulity typical of these characters, by stimulating our impatience to *get on with the story*, confirms our assent to the old maid's representational limits; indeed, as we ruthlessly skim their speeches, intolerable blemishes on a prose to which we otherwise gladly grant our undivided attention, we take the enforcement of these limits into our own hands. Never are we meant to see Emma as more of an "imaginist" than when she seeks to prove to Harriet the acceptability of being a rich old maid, and even here, she retains a formidable reality check: "If I thought I should ever be like Miss Bates!. . . I would marry to-morrow!" Besides this temporary self-delusion, nothing contests the common sense of Harriet's opinion: "To be an old maid at last . . . that's so dreadful!" (E 84–85).

And her opinion holds not merely for the world of the novels, where Emma blithely asserts that wealth alone can spare an old maid from being "the proper sport of boys and girls" (85), or where the Lucas boys are happy to be relieved, even by Mr. Collins, "from their apprehension of Charlotte's dying an old maid" (PP 122). It holds equally for the world in which the novels were written; there even Austen's growing renown did not prevent the stigma of spinsterhood from marking her brow alongside the laurels. "A friend of mine who visits her now," wrote Mary Russell Mitford in 1815, "says that [Austen] has stiffened into the most perpendicular, precise, taciturn piece of 'single blessedness' that ever existed."[21] This famous judgment is our only surviving personal impression of Austen that doesn't come from her friends and relations; and while its nastiness is unlikely to have been typical, its facility does suggest how promptly, where dislike did exist, Austen's "single blessedness" might be taken as the royal road to expressing it. But just as the Barthesian Neuter refuses to see itself in the glass of either the wretched castrato or the oppressed social existence of its homosexual author, so the Austen Neuter achieves a double nonrecognition, the objects of which are the fictive old maid who figures in the novels and the real old maid who has written them. In no way representing herself, the latter performs the disappearing act of Absolute Style instead; in Jane Austen no less than Robert Ferrars, the condition for the development of style is a subject (a self, a topic) with *almost nothing to say for itself*, and this "almost nothing" corresponds to a social abjection that, but for this powerful feat of indifference to it, the stylothete would have to suffer.

In one sense, of course, the stylothete suffers it anyway: not just, on the one side of Style, from those who don't get it, and hence all the more easily spot the woman, or the old maid, who is its ventriloquist; but equally, on the other side, from those who get it perfectly well, and hence all the more easily detect the fissures in its will to abstraction. When the poor in cultural capital make the same observation about Style that the best-educated and closest readers put all their subtlety in the service of confirming; when ignorant boys, who, without ever having read her, already know that reading Jane Austen is for girls and sissies, keep such high company as Charlotte Brontë, who once called Austen's writing the work of "an incomplete woman," or E. M. Forster, who called it "auntish," then what chance does Style ever have of keeping the would-be secret that is the damaged social identity from which it originates, and to which, like an impostor who must be stripped of his false beard, it is forever being routinely reduced?

In fact, however, it stands an excellent chance, since this reduction *can never be sure of itself*; quintessentially exasperated, even a bit panicked, it grows in vehemence with its increasing sense that its work is never done for good. The fascination of Style—call it, with a character in Hitchcock, the fascination of "looking into a mirror and seeing nothing but the mirror"—always returns to require another effort to anchor it. For however often we puts the screws to Style—"We already know where you came from! There's no point in refusing to tell us!"—we can never extort from it an actual confession. This is, finally, the wisdom possessed by Bersani's clever queen: Style never argues—hence can never actually lose the argument—for its freedom from contingency. Like Mary Crawford, who "would only smile and assert" (MP 96), it simply assumes the form of such freedom and hence, along with it, the incontestable reality granted, sustained, inhabited by whoever receives this form. Jane Austen's novels will never state what is widely supposed, or at least widely required, to be obvious: that their author is a woman, and an old maid. Though this refusal is responsible for the vigor of the punishing insistence that "she is so!" it is also the means whereby Austen Style achieves what we might call cultural *valence*: an ability not just to attract marginal or malformed subjects who need to take shelter in an image of universality and absoluteness, but also to combine with central ideological elements of a culture invested in such an image for itself. Always being defeated, always being remanded to social hell, Style nonetheless remains invincible, like the gay runner who, though damned for all eternity to doing laps around a track of burning sand, still imposes himself, even on Dante, as the winner of a race, not the loser.

II

Whoever wishes to illustrate Austen Style regularly gravitates toward the maxim, assuming that the perfection of this Style is highest, most visible and delectable, in bite-size form. Yet no sooner do we examine this practice of exemplification at any of its numerous sites—literary criticism, journalism, famous-quotation anthologies, the Lilliputian volumes of "The Wit and Wisdom of Jane Austen" for sale at the counter of certain gift shops—than we notice that it apparently suffers from a *dearth of good examples.* How else to explain why, so often, there seems to be only one such example: the first sentence of *Pride and Prejudice* (which, in a pardonable lapse, William Prichard once called the first sentence of Jane Austen); or why, at other times, as if under counsel by despair, the obiter dicta of a deluded Emma Woodhouse, or of some other equally ironized character, are offered as Austen's own, to fill out a presumably otherwise meager chrestomathy? However thoughtless, this tendentious practice correctly recognizes the formative apprenticeship of Austen Style to the eighteenth-century periodical essay developed in the papers of Steele, Addison, Goldsmith, and above all Johnson; the tradition was still so strong a reference in the Austen household that two of Jane's own brothers chose to continue it in a paper of their own called *The Loiterer.* Yet the practice also actively ignores—would the perfection of Austen Style be more safely preserved by such unknowing?—not just the fact, but the strangeness of the fact, that Austen Style elects to express itself in, of all things, a *narrative* form. The microstructure of this Style, its prose, may be the Johnsonian sentence or period, but its macrostructure, its genre, is no more the essay Austen learned to write from than it is either the character sketch (say, of Sir Roger de Coverley) or the *conte philosophique* (such as *Rasselas*) that were all this essay tradition ever generated in the way of narrative. Its genre is, as we all know, the Novel, a Novel, moreover, so fully fledged that even of those essayistic digressions in wide use by Austen's contemporary fellow novelists, her own fiction is (as she herself observed of *Pride and Prejudice*) almost too happily free.[22]

No doubt, thanks to the familiar divine attribute of omniscience, Austen's narration may still be thought to sustain as a whole the all-sufficiency of the epigrams that only sporadically spangle its pages. Still, by committing itself to that extensive representation of character and plot which is the Novel, Austen Style nonetheless alienates itself in a story-telling that, like the story told, must always have the *appearance* of incompletion, deferral, lack. And even if it be argued that this is only an appearance, a cloud to be dispelled by our eventual full recognition of the deity that has been in charge of everything all along, it remains puzzling that such a deity should choose to dramatize itself with this protracted game of veiling and revelation, absence and presence. Matters are stranger still; for in the course of its self-dramatization, this deity reveals a curious narcissism: Austen Style appears always to be telling us ... *about itself*, to have made style, small *s*, its most extensive and obsessive theme, equal to marriage. A female character can hardly be introduced without her being instantly placed in an intricately gradated relation to style or one or more of its stand-ins (elegance, wit, beauty, fashion). On first meeting Miss Tilney, for instance, we are told that "her air, though it had not all the decided pretension, the resolute stilishness of Miss Thorpe's, had more real elegance" (NA 55–56). We have seen this game being played

before at Mr. Gray's shop; just as Miss Thorpe's "resolute stilishness" is the foil for Miss Tilney's "real elegance," so the flash
of the one and the understatedness of the other collaborate to
set off the superior style of the narration that can so assess them
both. Already, then, we notice something less like narcissism
and more like the triumphalism supposed to compensate for a
narcissistic wound. Though Austen's typical heroines—Elizabeth Bennet, Mary Crawford, Emma Woodhouse—are all stylists, we are ceaselessly directed to observe the excesses, the failings, even the evils in their performance of style, as though the
stylothete were a queen bee who would tolerate no rivals. Not
content with merely observing the small s of their style, she
must actively belittle it, the better to persuade us that every
contest she wins has been no contest at all. Like the deity theorized by Austen's contemporary W.F.J. Schelling, a perfection
in perverse need of imperfection to assert itself,[23] or like the
God we already know, who has created nothing in His likeness,
but only Lucifers, who may not shine as bright, and Eves, who
must crave, but sicken from, a taste of the godhead, so the stylothete aims not simply at finding (her) Style *reflected* (as a con-
cern in the fictional world, or in the "real elegance" of a character) but at finding it reflected *in bad imitations.*

   Hence, contrary to the logic of its epigrammatism, Austen
Style finds its most congenial expression in the Novel, where it
splits into two mutually exclusive, and definitive, states of
being: (godlike) narration and (all-too-human) character. In
narration, this Style manifests itself as a consummate achievement, one which has so successfully obliterated the motives,
the process, the ends of its acquisition, that it requires supreme
critical finesse, or else the utmost stupidity, even to suggest
that any of these might once have existed. But in character—
in Elizabeth Bennet, in Mary Crawford, in Emma Woodhouse—the same Style is only a consummation to be wished,

an aspiration that is always dramatically induced, and eventually even more dramatically checked, by the specific contents and contexts to which it would affect indifference. Whereas Style-as-narration seems to come from nowhere but its own unconditioned freedom of mind, and to no purpose but to enjoy that freedom, style-as-character (no less than character itself, of which style, small *s*, would name only one among numerous other attributes) must be seen as the outcome of various social and psychological determinisms.

For instance, what Elizabeth calls her "impertinence," and we her wit, draws the chief of its energies from a plainly visible psychic process of denial, the denial of everything in her vulgar, dysfunctional family and its imperiled economic position, that makes her situation needful, awkward, embarrassing, humiliating, even outright abusive. And this denial also serves as the principal tool, however unconsciously Elizabeth uses it as such, of a social ambition whose object is the only one allowed to women in Austen: marrying up. "He has a very satirical eye," Elizabeth observes of Darcy early on in *Pride and Prejudice*, "and if I do not begin by being impertinent myself, I shall soon grow afraid of him" (PP 24). Yet, as everybody knows, Darcy does *not* possess a very satirical eye—he is far too stiff for that—and Elizabeth is projectively mistaking him for the only person she knows who does have such an eye, namely, her own father, who is continually casting it, to disdainful effect, on the female members of his household. This slip into blindness on the part of one usually so observant points to what is implicitly being repeated here: the whole by no means traceless process through which Elizabeth has come to mimic her father's wit, so that she can avert its fearsome thrusts with what he commends as her "quickness" (5) and at the same time, by the flattery of this imitation, secure his "preference" of her over his other girls (4).[24]

In resorting to the same language of "impertinence" by which she managed, as Jane Gallop would understand it, the daughter's seduction, Elizabeth has not just the acknowledged motive of forfending Darcy's supposedly cutting foil, but also the unconscious desire, which everyone but the two of them perceives, to flirt with him and win him over. Like the wardrobe of a Balzacian arriviste, carefully chosen to suggest that its wearer already enjoys the status it is the means of achieving, so from the start Elizabeth's style presumes all the freedom from need, the severance from vulgarity, that it eventually secures her in fact as mistress of Pemberley. She may be unaware of this connection at first—indeed, she must be, for otherwise the asceticism of style, its inflexible renunciation of the Person, would be a mere ruse, a tactic to be dropped as soon as it succeeded, another example, worthy of Miss Bingley, of those mean "arts which ladies sometimes condescend to employ for captivation" (40). But the narration never allows *us* to be equally in the dark. When, at Sir William's urging, Darcy asks to dance with her, Elizabeth gives him, instead of her hand, a sample of her style: first, she makes a decorous, but pointed dig ("Mr. Darcy is all politeness"); then, she throws him an arch look to make sure he gets it; and finally, in what is style's consummating gesture, that of closure, *she turns away*, as if Darcy and his requirements, like her and her needs, no longer existed. Nonetheless, "her resistance had not injured her with the gentleman," who on the contrary finds himself "thinking of her with some complacency"—in Austen's English, amiability, not smugness (27). And by the end of the novel, after the trick has been done, Elizabeth too can begin to recognize how it worked, that what "roused" Darcy, as she candidly puts it, was her refusal to court him, to be like the despised women "who were always speaking and looking, and thinking for [his] approbation alone." "Did you admire me for my impertinence?" "For the liveliness of your mind, I did" (380).

For a character, then, style seems to have considerable use; simply by virtue of *being* the brilliant solitaire set off and apart, Elizabeth also comes to *have* the wedding band that betokens the requisite bonds of full socialization. Style, it would seem, can get a girl married, provided only that she persuade herself into believing she is not using it to that end, or to any end but its own. In fact, though, the relation of style to the marriage plot is far more perverse than such an account suggests. Though the heroine's adoption of style may *induce* the court-ship plot, what brings this plot to fruition—what gets *her* desire to quicken, too—is a moment of mortification when, the better to acquire the selfhood she had never before wanted, the hero-ine *forsakes* style; or rather, what is much more demeaning, she flattens it into a merely decorative reminiscence of itself, like a flower pressed into a wedding album. If at first the novel allows for the naive belief in a happy match between style and the social (Elizabeth: "I hope I never ridicule what is wise or good" [57]), its subsequent development of both terms requires, if not their divorce on grounds of mutual incompatibility, then an emphatic subordination of style to the social, analogous to the strange, but perfectly ordinary, kind of "equal" marriage that Mr. Bennet recommends for Elizabeth—and that she gets—in which she will look up to her husband as her superior (376).[25] Ultimately, Elizabeth not only admits her eponymous "prejudice" against Darcy, but also lays the blame for it directly at the door of her wit: "I meant to be uncommonly clever in taking so decided a dislike to him, without any reason. It is such a spur to one's genius, such an opening for wit to have a dislike of that kind. . . . [O]ne cannot be always laughing at a man without now and then stumbling on something witty" (225–26). So she falls out of the universality of Austen Style—

the days of wit and retorts simply pass away—into the particularity of a self hitherto so hidden, so unknown, so barely ex-
isting that the pains she now takes to become acquainted with
it almost suggest the labor pains of giving it actual birth.

This fall—pivotal in Austen's major work, as everyone has
seen, without agreeing on just how—accomplishes three things;
or rather, what it accomplishes may be described in three distinct (if mutually dependent) registers. First, in the register of
style, it rudely aborts whatever ambition the heroine has har-
bored to Absolute Style; in no way now may her story be taken
to allegorize that Style's coming to be.[26] Concomitantly, in the
register of genre, this rupture of whatever continuity had ob-
tained, or might have been imagined, between the stylist and
the stylothete, only reinforces the division of functions internal
to the Novel. With Elizabeth or Emma now drawing herself
back inside the lines, the Austen Novel crystallizes that unal-
loyed antithesis between narration and character which even
now makes it look like the Platonic form from which every
later nineteenth-century English novel has both derived and
declined. And finally, in the register of the social, the heroine's
confirmation as a character carries out the sentence that her
style, so long as it survived, had hindered from being executed:
she becomes Woman at last, compelled both to accept the state
of lack that makes her a well-functioning subject, and to represent this lack to men so that, at her expense, they may imagine
themselves exempt from it.

And yet, for one whom this fall thus triply puts in her place,
the Austen heroine is curiously eager to give up style, and without regret or remorse at having done so. However many *readers*
lament the loss, *she* never even experiences it as one. About
her presumed deprivation of Darcy or Knightley, she may be
miserable and depressed indeed, but as for style, she forfeits it
unmourned. Nor does it at any time afterward make a ghostly

return (in the frequent way of an unmourned forfeiture) to haunt the freshly constructed subject with the painful dispossession that has made her one. No doubt, the heroine's failure to register any sacrifice here would make obvious sense if she were being hugely remunerated for it—if style were being discarded in order to become a subject in the position of, say, Mrs. Darcy, complete with copious pin money and real jewels. As Emma bitterly notes in her own case, "there would be no need of *compassion* to the girl who believed herself loved by Mr. Knightley" (E 408). At the moment of her mortification, though, neither Elizabeth nor Emma is cutting any such sweetheart deal. The former only trades in style for a subject that is "blind, partial, prejudiced, absurd" (PP 208); the latter, for one that is improper, inconsiderate, indelicate, irrational, unfeeling, vain, arrogant—in brief, deserving of "every bad name in the world" (E 408). Each has exchanged her ambition to Absolute Style for a self of which, in the very first moment of coming to know it, she is "absolutely ashamed" (PP 208). And overshadowing the moral reasons she brings forward to account for this shame—her misjudgment or misconduct—is the chagrin of being a woman who has just discovered that she *does* need to marry, and that she cannot—cannot, at any rate, marry that "ideal husband" who, as Wilde understood, is the only imaginable choice of a woman alive to the dimensions of her social privation. In a word, the Austen heroine chooses to embark on life as a person who already displays in ovo the most dreadful features of Miss Bates. Like some suddenly disenchanted princess who assumes, as her authentic form, that of a toad unlikely *ever* to be kissed, she gives up style to become the "bad subject" style had for a time held in abeyance.

I don't think that the strange affect attending the Austen heroine's mortification—her unaffected indifference to the loss of Absolute Style, her positive zeal to become the abject subject—is simply an emotional mystification that helps a woman bear the loss entailed on her social integration, and even prefer it to anything else. It seems at least as true to say that such affect accurately registers a sudden dialectical swing within the objects being exchanged: style, from being the sign of "the thing," devolves into the sign of the lack of the thing; while the self, with all its lacerations, becomes the source of a weird new strength and exuberance. And yet how could such a metamorphosis happen? and why should it happen just when it does?

How it happens has everything to do with the hidden but unbroken intimacy that the heroine's style has maintained with shame. It is not the paradox it appears that shame should be the thing that finally "gets to" style, which, though it has regularly served as the stylist's best defense against shame, may now without exaggeration be said to die of it. For all along shame has been style's encrypted alter ego—its alternate form *as ego*—and style, the unremitting labor of managing and masking this encryption. When in her best vulgar manner, and right in front of Darcy, Mrs. Bennet is chattering away about the verses a former admirer wrote on Jane ("and very pretty they were"), Elizabeth "impatiently" begins to sparkle: "I wonder who first discovered the efficacy of poetry in driving away love!" (44). And no sooner is she done than she starts to "tremble lest her mother should be exposing herself again," and longs to produce another conversational gem to dazzle and distract with (45). Though style has never exactly been an art that conceals *art*, it has certainly been an art that tries hard to conceal *labor*—in particular, as this incident nicely attests, the labor of shame management. Through every performance of style, there runs a hidden conduit that draws the flow of shame from the stylist at one end to someone or something else at the other (here, from Elizabeth to the hapless poetaster) but that between these openings may always leak or block up, and so is in constant need of maintenance and repair. (It is the ever-present possibility of a *reversion* of shame that occasionally allows the stylist to experience her style paranoiacally, as its victim; thus Lady Susan, whose brilliant "command of Language" has so easily worked on almost all the characters around her, comes to this bizarre, almost insane conclusion: "I . . . have been too easily worked on" [MW 251, 308].) If the collapse of style can follow so swiftly on its shaming—is it even a minute after Mr. Knightley rebukes Emma's "insolent . . . wit" that her cheeks flood with unchecked tears?—this is because style has always contained within itself a sort of fifth column, the extraordinary sensitivity to shame that is its basic operating equipment. In the instant of being shamed, style learns that (as we say of a fashion mistake) it isn't working. And if it isn't, then why not drop the tense—Austen would say *arch*—mode of abjection that is style in favor of the simpler mode of abjection that is the self? So intrinsically does shame control belong to the experience of style (on the part of practitioner, victim, and spectator alike) that to abandon style means leaving behind the whole structure of damage-and-reparation that style has been much too expensively keeping up. Small wonder that the Austen heroine never looks back at the departing shade of style; in ceding this ultimately futile weapon, she has simultaneously disburdened herself of a heavy chore: that of always having to be light, "to laugh, when she would rather have cried" (PP 364).

Yet if style had always contained the flammable components that now suddenly cause it to explode, didn't the container used to be sufficiently strong to take the heat? After all, Mr. Knightley had been trying to shame Emma from the very beginning, and she had always foiled his attempts with proto-Wildean brio. Let him play the card of truth when she claims to have made the match between the Westons: "You made a lucky guess; and *that* is all that can be said." She trumps it with the higher card of pleasure: "And have you never known the pleasure and triumph of a lucky guess?—I pity you.—I thought you cleverer" (E 13). Given such typical resilience, why does censure finally take so devastating a toll on style? Let me suggest that what in the end overtakes Emma's style, despite all the godlike or proverbial timelessness to which its utterances lay claim, is nothing less than a sense of its temporality—a temporality measured not against the large, event-filled scale of world-historical time, but in that minor unit of social pressure within which the Novel typically begins and ends: the time of a *generation*, from youth to eventual settlement. It is no accident that Emma discovers the folly of believing herself "in the secret of every body's feelings" amid a flurry of just-announced or anticipated engagements. When everyone of her age was single, she might embrace the role of the girl-who-will-never-get-married with spirit. Let her peers busy themselves with finding a husband; she would not, she need not. "She always declares she will never marry," Mr. Knightley had remarked of her early on, "which, of course, means just nothing at all" (41). In any event, at that point in the story, it was not obliged to mean anything at all; everyone Emma's age was also single, whether they were disposed to get married or not. But with Jane Fairfax engaged, and Harriet convinced she is about to be, Emma is now forcefully reminded that she has reached the marrying time in life. This time past, this window closed, and her generation of women divided accordingly into wives and old maids, her style *would have a different look*: no longer the exhilarating refusal of what she didn't need, it would begin to appear a pathetic substitution for what, in any case, she could no longer get. It is through this sharp new pressure of generation that the conjugal imperative now speaks to Emma so loudly, and the link of style to shame—to the shame of shames, which is the unconsummated relation to the marriage plot—now becomes so intolerably visible. (Elizabeth's comparable crisis is not, of course, so concentrated, but she enjoys the advantage of having been early and expressly warned that, once such supreme shame is recognized for any part of the compound, the elixir of style tastes like a distillate of sour grapes. "Take care, Lizzy," Mrs. Gardiner had said on receiving her niece's sardonic appraisal of young men; "that speech savours strongly of disappointment" [PP 154].)

Inevitably, then, at the same moment the heroine shrinks from style, she feels the sudden excitement of a desire long held in abeyance, but now, thanks to this intensified stimulation, materializing from almost nothing into colossal proportions, like the magic tent in the *Arabian Nights*: the desire *to be a Person*. The demeaned condition she formerly did everything in her power not to inhabit, she now shows an interest, an eagerness, even an enjoyment in coming to know, and getting to perform. And whatever sadism may be motivating the stylothete, it is not finally masochism that drives the stylist to trade style for self. Certainly, in the drama of choosing to be a Person, the protagonist never chooses anything but the Person *notwithstanding*: the Person in spite of the still manifest faults and failings, dreads and dangers, intrinsic to the state of being one. Emma must take on "all the perturbation that such a developement of self, such a burst of threatening evil, such a confusion of sudden and perplexing emotions, must create," the appositions pointedly explaining what a development of self entails (E 409). But, if by nothing else, the pain of this choice is simultaneously soothed—compensated—rewarded by the prestige of its own heroics. Think of all the truisms that, as though bestowing so many medals for bravery, the common wisdom endlessly pins to the choice of the Person: where in the world is it *not* believed that it is better to have a broken heart than none at all, to fail than not to have tried, to be someone instead of no one, and all the rest?

In this, Emma's bravura performance of the Person resembles nothing so much as the first-act finale of a Broadway musical: the sentimental spectacle of an injured subject whose injury makes her exultant, triumphant with all the power of that second injury which, by means of this very performance, *she has given herself.* Emma's self-inflicted wound stands as proof that flowing through her veins is an abundance, an excess, of that most precious of ideological fluids: Life, the Life under the aegis of which she reorients herself—"cost her what it would" (429)—toward the others who populate the communal scene, and toward the one in particular required to form with her a couple on that scene. In what Bersani has called our culture of redemption, the choice of the Person comes endorsed with a stamp of existential authenticity, affirming that it is the true and proper form for human being. What style had once feigned to be, the Person now is: its own reward.

But, as every reader knows, the Person too is an unavowed feint; even to Elizabeth or Emma, it doesn't come as a complete surprise that the usual ideological rewards for choosing the Person "for its own sake" should soon be followed by extraordinary material ones: that Mr. Darcy should propose a second time, or that Mr. Knightley should marry no one but Emma. Who doubts that, if these outcomes failed to occur, both heroines would be as sorely disappointed as Elinor before them, to discover "the difference between the expectation of an unpleasant event, however certain the mind may be told to consider it, and certainty itself" (SS 357). Through mists of denegation, for instance, the principle of hope shines brightly forth from the lowest depths of Emma's personal abasement: "In spite of all her faults, she knew she was dear to [Mr. Knightley]; might she not say, very dear?—When the suggestions of hope, however, which must follow here, presented themselves, she could not presume to indulge them" (E 415). But though "she had no hope, nothing to deserve the name of hope" (416), the name keeps being used to silhouette a prospect that does deserve it. In the very next clause, Emma entertains "the hope (at times a slight one, at times much stronger) that Harriet might . . . be overrating [Mr. Knightley's] regard," and a few pages later, "the hope that [time would find her] more rational, more acquainted with herself" (423)—in plainer words, "more worthy of him, whose intentions and judgments had been ever so superior to her own" (475).

Style, then, gets you the things it fools you into thinking you don't want, but only, finally, by being abandoned for the Person, which makes you *know* you want them. As a theme, or represented practice, in Austen's work, style is typically obedient to this dialectic of its eventual dispensability. It wards off the Mr. Collinses or Mr. Eltons only until such time as it has captivated a Mr. Darcy or a Mr. Knightley, when it can and must be dropped to secure him. If, in the first moment of this dialectic, the heroine vanishes into style, in the second she precipitates out of it, not as the malformed and all but unrepresentable creature that, but for the initial intervention of style, she should have feared being, but as the Person in glory, the person who is, like Emma in Mr. Knightley's final vision of her, "faultless in spite of all her faults" (433) and whose faultlessness and faults alike are complemented in the "perfect happiness" of a married union. (The redemption of particularity in Jane Austen: being particular *with another person*.)[27]

That most readers have found this dialectic charming in its operation, and not cynical, is no doubt owing to the heroine's twofold naiveté. The heroine no more sees her exercise of style as a means of social ambition than she recognizes her eventual choice of the Person over style as an advanced moment in the same process. Only because she has elected first style, and then the Person, for their intrinsic value do they work thus in tandem to win her more than that; and this law—the law, as we might call it after René Girard, of the Twice Feigned Askesis—

is given the appearance of operating by sheer fortuity: the heroine's plot takes its definitive turns in default of her deliberate plotting. And it is the heroine's good conscience that sustains our culture's bad faith in relation to a marriage plot that is, in fact, usually *arranged* in just this fancifully spontaneous way.

But suppose that somebody, for whatever reason, failed to follow the dialectic of style all the way to its disappearance in the Person fit for coupling? Suppose somebody persisted in not acknowledging the shame of style, and so remained stranded in it? Of such arrested development, of course, Mary Crawford is a famous case in point. In essence, she receives the same sort of rebuke from Edmund as Emma does from Mr. Knightley, but her response, at least as Edmund recalls it, couldn't be more different:

> She was astonished, exceedingly astonished—more than astonished. I saw her change countenance. She turned extremely red. I imagined I saw a mixture of many feelings—a great, though short struggle—half a wish of yielding to truths, half a sense of shame—but habit, habit carried it. She would have laughed if she could. It was a sort of laugh as she answered, "A pretty good lecture upon my word. Was it part of your last sermon? At this rate, you will soon reform every body at Mansfield and Thornton Lacey; and when I hear of you next, it may be as a celebrated preacher in some great society of Methodists, or as a missionary into foreign parts."
> (MP 458)

Mary does more than illustrate the arrested dialectic of style; she espouses it, with the consequence that it may well be all she ever will espouse. Left "long in finding" a satisfactory husband (469)—a period that, as far as we readers are concerned, lasts forever—she is the saint and martyr of Austen Style. If she scorns to confess the pathology of her style, she must suffer all its now greatly augmented pathos, for the marrying season is approaching its end, and all the good men seem to have been caught. In her choice of style over self—a choice that, once definitive, entails her virtual disappearance as a character—she adumbrates the fate of that still more famous prisoner of Style, the stylothete herself. No doubt, from the standpoint of Absolute Style, the Austen heroine couldn't help wearing the aspect of a wannabe who finally had the good sense to give up a career in the style business for marriage and a family. But now, from the no less absolute vantage of "perfect happiness" (E 484), it is Austen Style that looks deficient: the secret dependency of perfection on imperfection, of narration on character, seems motivated less by a desire to affirm the superiority of the narrative voice, than by the endless fascination of that voice with the thing that it has foregone in order to speak. From the secure shores where the complete, the coupled character has finally landed, we no longer look up at a vainglorious god, or even at a vengeful one. What we glimpse is more curious, if not less paradoxical: a supreme being who, though solitary, though single, has made "perfect happiness" depend on entering the condition of the couple, and is now regarding this paradise from outside its gates. Recall the character in Wilde who, finding herself with an incriminating diamond bracelet on her arm, is unable to get it off: she tears at it to no purpose, unless it be the further mortification of her delicate flesh. But what is Lady Cheveley's frantic despair, is Austen's rigorous parti pris. In full knowledge that the bracelet, as it were, is also a bondage, she makes no attempt to remove it; unlike many another jewel in nineteenth-century fiction, there will be no losing this one. And unlike many a stylothete after her, Austen will grant no final concession to the social, to its demeaning little image of her, make no belated return to a particularity of which, so late in the day, nothing would be left but crotchets and crow's feet.

In Wilde's *De Profundis* or Barthes's "Soirées de Paris," the author's long starved appetite for representation, any representation whatsoever, at last drives him to depict his own abjection. In Austen, so completely does her subject remain the negation of her subjectivity that, even when she is most seriously ill, she elects to write about hypochondria. Nothing since has approached (her) Style in the stringency of its refusal to realize its author personally, of its commitment to absent her from a representation where, with no chance of even coming close to what counts as "perfect happiness," she could find only stigma.

Near the start of this chapter, I observed that Austen Style not only knew whereof it spoke, but also spoke without any apparent experiential implication in such knowledge. I called this the paradox of divine omniscience, but we might now see it as, also, the paradox of divine melancholy, in which an impersonal deity unceasingly contemplates the Person that is its own absolutely foregone possibility. This melancholy will be the subject of my final chapter, where I'll be locating it not in its thematic manifestations—say, in the extravagantly rueful *Persuasion*—for these, it seems to me, represent a degree of expressiveness appreciably at odds with both melancholy's inability to mourn and Austen Style's unwillingness to do so. Rather, I'll be locating it as it determines, or is determined by, two deep-structural phenomena: one, quite well known already, is the unprecedented prominence of free indirect style in *Emma*; and the other, not at all known, or even identified, is what I shall be calling, quite presumptuously, the *faults* of style that abound in *Sanditon*. Both, I hope, will take us further into this secret of Austen Style: that the stylothete harbors a hidden wish—of whose impossible fulfillment she has made an absolute refusal—to renounce the renunciation that makes her one.

THREE   Broken Art

I

Picture, if you can, a past moment of literary criticism when, institutionally empowered and rewarded, close reading was the critic's chief tool of professional advancement; his command of a *text*, his capacity to tease from it a previously invisible *nuance*, or illuminate it under a fresh *insight*, would as good as light the pipe in his mouth and sew elbow patches on his jacket, so unfailingly did he thus distinguish himself as the compleat, the full professor of English Literature. Now picture, if you need to, a future moment of literary criticism in which the same practice has fallen into total dereliction, and the *esprit de finesse* has ceded all its previous authority and prestige to the *esprit de géométrie*, more familiarly known as "theory." Even more efficiently than it once promoted its practitioner through the ranks of the professoriat, close reading now transforms him into an emeritus, antiquated and rambling, but not—alas for his pride!—too deaf to hear the resounding impatience of his audience that he get to the point, to the paradigm, which has become the only object of their peremptory, poverty-stricken desire. I don't mean to suggest by either exercise that, whether or not we ever lived in such a past, we should contemplate returning to it, or that, if such a future is indeed at hand, we should do our best to resist it. On the contrary, it is close reading in its humbled, futile, "minoritized" state that would win my preference in any contest. For only when close reading has lost its respectability, has ceased to be the slave of mere convenience, can it come out as a thing that, even under the high-minded (but now somewhat kitschy-sounding) rationales of its former mission, it had always been: an almost infantile desire to be *close*, period, as close as one can get, without literal plagiarism, to merging with the mother-text. (In an essay once, citing the first sentence of *Pride and Prejudice*, I left out the quotation marks.) But the point of picturing these two extreme conditions is not to get us to choose sides, but to recognize that, if we retain any vital relation to close reading whatsoever, as we all do, we must always be on both. For the practice of close reading has always been radically cloven: here, on one side, my ambition to master a text, to write *over* its language and refashion it to the cut of my argument, to which it is utterly indifferent; there, on the other, my longing to write *in* this language, to identify and combine with it. The adept in close reading must assert an autonomy of which he must also continually betray the weak and easily overwhelmed defenses.

These remarks on close reading may provide a metaphor, drawn from the homely lives of literary critics who don't write novels, for the fantasmatics of that technique of *close writing* that Austen more or less invented for the English novel, and which is *le style indirect libre*, or free indirect style. Ferguson has regretted the suggestive terminological affinity between free indirect style and style *tout court*, as leading us to link the device "with the unanalyzable notion of style rather than with the more substantial notion of representable form."[28] But of all traditional English novelists, Austen has long served us as the most striking example of both notions: of that self-evident secret which is Style, and that widely diffused representational technology known as the Novel. And the present essay has above all attempted to argue the inter-implication of the formal accomplishment of the Austen Novel, which matches uniquely impersonal narration to equally unprecedentedly rounded characters, and the fantasmatic achievement of Austen Style, as it bursts upon us (no matter how often or extensively we encounter it) in all the archaic authority of personal sourcelessness. We last left the secret of Style at this: that the stylothete harbors a hidden wish—of whose impossible fulfillment she has made an absolute refusal—to renounce the renunciation that makes her one. Let us now add the specification that it is above all in free indirect style, where the wish and refusal are most nearly joined, that this secret is kept and told.

The significance of free indirect style for Austen Style is not that it attenuates the stark opposition between character and narration, much less abandons it, but that it performs this opposition *at ostentatiously close quarters.* In free indirect style, the two antithetical terms stand, so to speak, as close as possible to the bar (the virgule, the disciplinary rod) that separates them. Narration comes as near to a character's psychic and linguistic reality as it can get without collapsing into it, and the character does as much of the work of narration as she may without acquiring its authority. Though free indirect style plainly offers *a third term* between character and narration, it is, or means to be, a nondialectical one: a kind of turnstile that helps organize the boundary, and recycle the binary, of an antithesis. Organize? Say rather flaunt: free indirect style gives a virtuoso performance, against all odds, of the narration's persistence in detachment from character, no matter how intimate the one becomes with the other. And its most daredevil feats do not occur where the narration is representing the consciousness of a fool like Sir Walter Elliot, or a cheapskate like John

Dashwood, instances where the difference between narration and character is manifest at too many levels to be jeopardized even if both came to acquire the same ontological status. No, such feats occur when, in the course of vainly aspiring to narration, a character in turn inspires it with an equally impossible desire to renounce its condition for her own, as a fully representable person; in other words, in a case where it seems that if the structural bar of antithesis ever slipped away—which it never does—its place would be immediately taken by a mirror. For, no less than close reading, the close writing that is free indirect style is also given over to broaching an impossible identification. In the paradoxical form of an impersonal intimacy, it grants us at one and the same time the experience of a character's inner life as she herself lives it, and an experience of the same inner life as she never could. Though the irony that thus always accompanies free indirect style necessarily severs the identification with character, it nonetheless still presupposes it as one of its terms. Indeed, only in being severed, "lost," does this identification acquire fantasmatic force; only at the point of no return does it come back as a haunting apparition.

There is, of course, only one such case; her name is Emma Woodhouse. That some singularly intense authorial cathexis lodges in this character, Jane Austen has informed us herself: "I am going to take a heroine whom no one but myself will much like" (M 157). By which, Austen does not mean to say that Emma is unlikable—an opinion from which countless generations of readers have dissented, just as they were supposed to. She is simply putting us on notice that no one can ever like Emma so well as her author. The name itself goes a long way to measuring just how well; even before it christened Miss Woodhouse, it had already enjoyed the privilege of being the name Austen most frequently chose for her heroines. In the juvenilia, as her biographer Park Honan has noted, Austen used the name Emma "with such affection that her parents might have wondered why they ever called her Jane."[29] To his list of examples—Emma Marlowe in "Leslie Castle"; Emma Marlow in "Edgar and Emma"; Emma Harley in "The Adventures of Mr. Harley"; Emma Stanhope in "Sir William Mountague"— we may add Emma Watson in "The Watsons" and the jokey stipulation in Austen's late "Plan of a Novel" that "the name of the work *not . . .* be *Emma*" (MW 430). For reasons of state— of Style, that is—Austen normally gives scant license to "the play of the signifier" in her novels, but the name Emma stands out as an exception. "What two letters of the alphabet are there, that express perfection?" Mr. Weston propounds. "M. and A.— Em—ma.—Do you understand?" (E 371).[30] We understand even more, as we see the name—*aimé* indeed—reforming itself all over the text: not just *abbreviated* (as M.A.), but also *replicated* (in "little Emma," Emma's niece); *inverted* (into "Anne," Mrs. Weston's first name); *crossed* (with "Anne" to yield "Anna," the child that Mrs. Weston thus seems to have had by Emma rather than Mr. Weston); and *extended* (into "my Emma," which, as a mode of one character's addressing another, is unparalleled in Austen's novels, and even here is employed only by Mrs. Weston at her most maternal and Mr. Knightley after having become Emma's betrothed).[31] And, of course, Mr. Weston's lit- eralization of the name, harking back to the game of anagrams played earlier in the novel, invites us to search out words in all four of its letters. Whether we simply reverse the order of these, and find Flaubert before the fact ("Emma, c'est moi"), or vari- ously draw out of them the twinned themes of narcissism and maternity (me, ma, me-ma, ma-me, mame), the name already broaches the open secret of an impossible identification be- tween the No One who is narrating and the most fully charac- terized Person in all Austen.

Free indirect style in *Emma* having been the subject of count- less discussions, I confine my own to a single extraordinary moment in the novel: the passage that straddles the end of book

II, chapter 2, and the beginning of book II, chapter 3 (169–70).
In II, 2, on meeting Jane Fairfax after a long absence, Emma
recognizes, as though for the first time, her extraordinary
beauty: "her face—her features—there was more beauty in
them all together than she had remembered" (167). And this
beauty, so much the more forceful in its impression on Emma
for having rectified her earlier mistake, and awakened her from
previous oblivion, prompts her to feel that she has "injured"
Jane by her "past prejudices and errors." "In short, she sat,
during the first visit, looking at Jane Fairfax with twofold complacency; the sense of pleasure and the sense of rendering justice, and was determining that she would dislike her no longer"
(167). It is quite as though the text were exemplifying Elaine
Scarry's contention that an encounter with beauty—most pow-
erfully when it catches us by surprise—disposes us toward
being just.[32] But beauty in Jane Austen, like the beauty *of* Jane
Austen, does not embody the plenitude and inclusiveness either
of Scarry's ideal or of Scarry's own enchanting style of argu-
mentation. On the contrary, as I've already suggested, the ach-
ing beauty of Austen Style has everything to do with the fact
that it invites and sustains in whoever encounters it an invidi-
ous fantasy of plenitude and *ex*clusiveness. So, unsurprisingly,
on a second meeting, Emma finds that "these were charming
feelings—but not lasting" (168), as Jane's former provocations,
all amounting to forms and instances of *reserve*, have reap-
peared. Jane is disgustingly, is suspiciously reserved, Emma de-
cides; and if anything can be more, where all is most, she is
more reserved on the subject of Weymouth and the Dixons
than anything. The chapter ends thus:

> The like reserve prevailed on other topics. She and Mr.
> Frank Churchill had been at Weymouth at the same time. It
> was known that they were a little acquainted; but not a sylla-

ble of real information could Emma procure as to what he truly was. "Was he handsome?"—"She believed he was reckoned a very fine man." "Was he agreeable?"—"He was generally thought so." "Did he appear a sensible young man; a young man of information?"—"At a watering place, or in a common London acquaintance, it was difficult to decide on such points. Manners were all that could be safely judged of, under a much longer acquaintance than they had yet had of Mr. Churchill. She believed every body found his manners pleasing." Emma could not forgive her. (169)

And here is how the following chapter begins:

Emma could not forgive her;—but as neither provocation nor resentment were discerned by Mr. Knightley, who had been of the party, and had seen only proper attention and pleasing behaviour on each side, he was expressing the next morning, being at Hartfield again on business with Mr. Woodhouse, his approbation of the whole; not so openly as he might have done had her father been out of the room, but speaking plain enough to be very intelligible to Emma. He had been used to think her unjust to Jane, and had now great pleasure in marking an improvement. (170)

You will have observed the strangeness of the same phrase being used both at the end of one chapter and at the beginning of the next, as though just for a moment, this impeccable Style, like an old-fashioned phonograph stylus, had got stuck in a groove, or as though the narrative machinery were experiencing a brief, but unprecedented technical malfunction in shifting gears. But the minor panic this moment provokes in us—what are we to make of it? how are we to read it?—lasts only until we understand we will never be asked to make anything of it, or to read it at all. It is, if anything, a stylistic mishap, irrelevant to the story that now proceeds in a soothing and total indifference to it. The inconsequence of this odd little repetition makes us overlook its startling weirdness, or more accurately, prevents us from retaining our sense of this weirdness. No wonder that, in a novel saturated in commentary—a commentary, moreover, by no means inhibited by a fear of the trivial or obvious—this strange feature has always passed with no more remark than Robert Ferrars's toothpick case; there seems to be nothing in it.

By way of breaking the silence, let me harp on the oddity of the moment. To my knowledge, it has no parallel in nineteenth-century fiction, but even if it did, it would still seem curiously out of place in Austen, where the usual justifications for a rhetoric of repetition—emphasis, clarity, the exigencies of transition—don't quite apply. After all, this is a world where it is only the stupid and the chattering who lack the sense not to repeat themselves; and this is a work in which a stern principle of concision shows no mercy in throwing overboard the redundancies elsewhere supposed to give narration needed ballast. Even supposing a legato effect were intended, it would invariably be spoiled on being obliged to leap the hurdle of a chapter break, which, like a fade-to-black in film, executes as strong an internal disconnect as the Novel has at its disposal. In an artist whose sentences frame everything with elegant edges, there is something unseemly, or clumsily seamed, about these borders.

This is, at any rate, one way of looking at it. But here is another. Once we examine each of the two identical sentences in the context of its respective paragraph, it becomes clear that a shift, a change, has occured in the time or space between them. During the chapter break, what had been the indirect and impersonal *performance* of Emma's consciousness has become the mere matter-of-fact *notation* of that thought. On its first occurrence, "Emma could not forgive her" mimics Emma's conscious if unreflective mood. By the time of the second, without a word being altered, the sentence has been distilled into what Ann Banfield calls a "fact of the fiction": a kind of stone on which Mr. Knightley is already stumbling in the scene that emerges.[33] What generates the first "Emma could not forgive her" is Emma's own affective consciousness, intimately accessed and ironically inflected by its free indirect narrative performance. What generates the second "Emma could not forgive her" is pure narration, a detached consciousness to which Emma's own has ceased to contribute, having been reduced to a little bit of information useful to the plot. By virtue of repeating the same formula (truly magical), we move from free indirect style—for all its irony, always grounded in an intimate identificatory relation to the image of a person—to mere omniscient narration, more remote in its detachment, and less engagé in its impersonality. What makes this shift worth our attention is neither that it *is* a shift, for such movements in and out of free indirect style happen all over *Emma*; nor that it is "undecidable," for I take it we all agree that we are further inside Emma on one side of the break and further removed from her on the other. It is the form that the shift takes here—a repetition across a chapter break—that makes it unique. For if we even recognize the difference in the repetition, we do so only belatedly, on looking back at it from the context that comes to be built around it. And this belatedness of perception only underscores the shift more heavily, as though, without being thus retrospectively startled by it, we might have overlooked it—as in fact, of course, at the actual moment it seems to have taken place (on the second occurrence of "Emma could not forgive her"), we already *must* have done.

Far from evincing a lapse in Austen's celebrated economy, the repetitive transition ends up being an awesome illustration of it: finally perceived, her adroit arrangement surprises us into discovering the difference between two narrative modes across one and the same phrase. Yet neither can this transition be reduced to the declaration of a purely formal mastery; the toothpick case, we know, is never entirely empty. Besides the stylistic fluency, then, we need to recognize the retardation, the hesitation, the reluctance, I should finally say the impossibility, so insistently dramatized in the transition. It is as though the narration were trying, and failing, to pull away from the attraction of free indirect style—from that identification with an image of the Person which is the only thing that distinguishes it, fantasmatically speaking, from its usual "omniscient" mode. But in the course of shaking off its secret, severed identification with Emma, it has produced a cloud of dust that only resettles on it, as the telltale residue of that same identification. It seems as hard for Jane Austen to relinquish her identificatory cathexis on Emma, or to cool it down into an even more detached form, as it is for Emma to relinquish her grudge against Jane Fairfax. In a way, of course, this cathexis is not simply *like* a grudge; it is itself a grudge, against the possibility that the stylothete is denied.

Why at bottom does Emma resent Jane Fairfax? "Mr. Knightley had once told her it was because she saw in her the really accomplished young woman, which she wanted to be thought herself" (166). "Emma could not forgive her/Emma could not forgive her": so Style flaunts its mastery, its ability to enter and then exit a character's state of mind at will, while always retaining, at whatever level of intimacy, the immunity of its impersonality. But so also Style avows how deeply, in a former life, it might have desired the identification with that full social being who, for all her faults, is faultless in the complete acceptability of her social representation: handsome, clever, rich, and, as everybody already knows, destined to be coupled too. It gazes in fascination on that identification from which, already discernibly detached, it must now pull back even further. "Emma could not forgive her/Emma could not forgive her": that is finally to say, Emma can never be *forgotten* by her, who is not Jane Fairfax but Jane Austen. After all, it is this Jane who, far more consistently than her namesake in the novel, exhibits "such coldness and reserve—such apparent indifference whether she pleased or not" (166); and who thus may be seen to acknowledge here the incontrovertible truth of what, under the *nom de guerre* of Fairfax, Emma can't bear in her. The melancholy of Austen Style lies not in the fact that its renunciation of the world—the renunciation that has allowed it to make a world—is never complete, but in the fact that its renunciation of the world may never be *in*complete, may never be modified or muted. What most argues the melancholy of the passage at hand is not the reluctance of the withdrawal, so much as the dry, wittily mechanical necessity of it. To a large extent, as I suggested in the first chapter, Austen's persistent moral condemnation of style—as by turns trivial, factitious, misleading, dangerous, evil—is a strategy of camouflage: shameful sign of the Woman, style must always be "over there," in Robert Ferrars's empty toothpick case. But surely what also motivates this condemnation is Style's own sense of the untruth in its exclusive self-sufficiency: the knowledge that with its constant and rigorous self-denial it does not simply counter a fear of reverting to the abject subject who would no longer have even the dubious protection of style; it also seeks to advance a dream that it might correspond to the plenitude of a Person. The beauty of Style, I have claimed, lies in the way it shuts out the world that would otherwise shut out the stylothete. This beauty, though, is also the melancholy of Style; its exclusive plenitude obliges Style always to harbor a dialectical reminder not just of that excluded self it had to give up, but also of that included self it never had, and so never *will* give up, for it is what we might properly call its ego ideal. Ultimately, then, Austen's God is not Schelling's, with the perverse need of perfection for imperfection; on the contrary, her deity presents one kind of perfection melancholically longing to be coupled with another. That is why, to anyone with the smallest sense of style, of Austen Style at any rate, *Emma* must be considered both the most perfect *and* the most melancholy of her novels, because here the perfection of Style, of No One, opens the secret of its impossible desire to possess the perfection of a Person who has, who is, everything. "Harriet was nothing . . . [Emma] was every thing herself" (430). Though Austen could not have known the Germanic origin of the name, the stylothete is full of appreciation—full of nothing, finally, but appreciation—for the fact that "Emma" means *whole*.

II

What I've been calling the melancholy of Style in Austen depends on the author's firm refusal to give (her) Style a human face. Yet it is the prospect of a yielding on just this point that is raised, even partly realized, in *Persuasion*, the great sentimental favorite in the Austen canon and, not coincidentally, the great false step of Austen Style. In the previous novels, the judgment pronounced against style in the sphere of character had in no way deterred the performance of Style embarked on by the narration. It was Elizabeth or Emma who came to renounce her presumption to style, and redeem herself personally in the process; for itself, the narration never ceased to uphold that presumption, affirming with each and every sentence its inhuman mastery of, as Gide put it, "everything that *can* be mastered." In *Mansfield Park*, for instance, where its thematic condemnation of style was harshest, the narration may have had the goodness to choose a heroine devoid of style, and the kindliness to shelter her under the cloak of its own eloquence and authority, but never did it dream of taking charity to the point of partaking in her self-mistrust, much less her linguistic indigence. Let Fanny enjoy the honor of always being what Elizabeth or Emma enjoys the honor of eventually becoming: her own person; the figure of Austen Style—the figure I've been calling the stylothete—remained No One. However deeply it peered down from its divine pinnacle to observe the somebodies below, it suffered no vertigo, struggled with no panic temptation to take the plunge into their midst. Yet in *Persuasion*, as if this resolutely melancholy figure had all of a sudden turned suicidal, it lets itself—and us too—contemplate the possibility of its falling into personification.

The fall is projected from both poles of Austen Style, narration and character. For its part, the narration is newly prone to throwing little fits of pique whose manifest source in *irritability* is a far cry from the nonchalant detachment that once pronounced truths universally acknowledged. Here, it suddenly bristles with contempt for the deceased Dick Musgrove and heaps ridicule on anyone foolish enough to mourn him and be fat in the bargain; and there, equally out of the blue, it flares up in annoyance with even Anne's pretty "musings of high-wrought love and eternal constancy" as "enough to spread purification and perfume" through all Bath (P 192). Such petulance confers on the narration not only an unwonted *personality*, but one, moreover, composed of some main traits of the typically conceived old maid, "illiberal and cross" (E 85). Yet it is not these sporadic outbursts which prove most decisive in suggesting the fall of *Persuasion*'s narration onto the terrain of the characterizable. If No One actually *sustains* such a fall here, it paradoxically does so under the aspect of the heroine herself, in what, as we'll see, is her unique absorption of Austen's narration. It was the novelist herself, of course, who first acknowledged the (troubling, lovable) anomalousness of Anne Elliot as a character. "You may *perhaps* like the Heroine," Austen wrote her niece, "as she is almost too good for me" (L 335). Absent the coyness that downplays the seriousness of its critical understanding, the comment broaches the two most important facts about Anne. The first is that she is too good for the novelist *as such*—in other words, that her character somehow confronts the Austen Novel with a certain problem, or possibility, which interferes with the usual functioning of its system. And the second is that it is precisely the strange dysfunction brought on by Anne that permits so many readers—and so extravagantly— to "like" her.

Part of Anne's singularity, no doubt, consists in her being so nearly irrevocably single. With her, we are finally given what in the previous novels had been regularly missing: a central and serious portrait of the spinster. Having broken off her engagement to Wentworth, refused Charles Musgrove, and effectively taken herself off the marriage market before the novel begins, Anne occupies the situation of the old maid from the very outset. Accordingly, she suffers the full social disregard attendant on this situation. She is "nothing" and "nobody" to so many people that her abjection seems systemic; the entire social world—the world of couples and families—is organized so as to be always giving her lessons in "the art of knowing [her] own nothingness" (P 42). But mortification is more than the daily bread of Anne's spinsterly social existence; for this Spartan diet she has developed so decided a taste that she has made it the basis of what Foucault would call "a practice of the self." With weird, almost wild jubilance, she seizes on external mortification as the occasion for a second, internal mortification that, with equal severity, she herself inflicts. When, for example, Wentworth's brutal words—"so altered that he should not have known her again!"—are repeated back to her, Anne "soon began to rejoice that she had heard them. They were of sobering tendency; they allayed agitation; they composed, and consequently must make her happier" (61). Even if free indirect style had wanted to ironize Anne's thoughts here—the determination to be happy not quite coinciding with happiness itself—the irony is hardly one that can have escaped her self-castigating consciousness.

Elsewhere, as we've sufficiently seen, Austen's narration, though claiming authority absolutely, affirms it relationally, as an epistemological advantage over character. When free indirect style mimics Emma's thoughts and feelings, it simultaneously inflects them into keener observations of its own; for our benefit, if never for hers, it identifies, ridicules, corrects all the secret vanities and self-deceptions of which Emma, pleased as Punch, remains comically unconscious. And this is generally what being a character in Austen means: to be slapped silly by a narration whose constant battering, however satisfying—or terrifying—to readers, its recipient is kept from even noticing. After all, how would even the cleverest character divine that he or she is *being narrated*?[34] But to this otherwise rhetorical question, Anne in fact provides a kind of answer. She disables the ironizing inherent in Austen's narration by having already conscripted it as a function of her own scathing self-intimacy. If she is too good for the novel's own good, then, this is not so much because she incarnates an excellence in which the narration finds little to put under its correction, as that she is always submitting herself to a similar correction in that daily practice of mortification through which she defines, fortifies, and even enjoys her sense of self.

The narration of *Persuasion*, then, can do little to Anne that she has not already done to herself. When she is "amused" to have preached "patience and resignation" to Captain Benwick, she makes—and so deprives the narration of making *about*

her—the "more serious reflection . . . that she had been elo-
quent on a point in which her own conduct would ill bear
examination" (101). And not only does such self-mortification
make her mistress of the free indirect style practiced on *her*,
still more extensively—"no one . . . so capable as Anne" indeed
(114)—it lets her appropriate to herself that practiced on others as well. Consider, from early in the novel: "Anne . . . was
nobody with either father or sister: her word had no weight;
her convenience was always to give way;—she was only Anne"
(5). A classic example of free indirect style, that last clause
mimics and mocks Anne's fatuous undervaluation by her near
relations. But who cannot feel the uncanny telepathy by which,
in its sheer cruelty, the sentence seems equally to have ema-
nated from Anne's own peculiar interiority, as we soon get to
know it? "These words," David Kurnick remarks, "have the in-
cantatory feeling, half sorrowful, half resentful, of a self-admin-
istered lesson," as if they originated with Anne's wish "to re-
mind herself of a harsh reality so as to steel herself against its
effects."[35] At such a moment, where the narration corresponds—and hence caters—to Anne's self-mortification, that
masterly third person which narration normally employs for
putting characters in their place palpably morphs into a *servile*
third person such as a maid might use in addressing her mistress: "Madame désire?" Through fully submitting "in silent,
deep mortification" (61), Anne has dragged the narration down
with her into an unprecedented relinquishment of its own cog-
nitive advantage. No longer quite distinguishable from the consciousness that it would otherwise be scoring points against,
the narration that has trained us to think of it as the total absence of Person must now seem, if not personified, *personifiable*, and if not personifiable in *any* person, then in the kind
of person, like Anne, whose consciousness has so thoroughly
internalized narration's ironizing effect *on* character that narra-

tion can seem, however eerily, to originate *with* character, like a diary written in the third person.

Granted, the portrait of Anne the Unmarried One is painted over upon her reunion with Wentworth, the always implicit prospect of which has allowed every reader to anticipate just this pentimento. And yet, even as that portrait is being retrofitted with a gold band, another devoted to the same subject is being sketched in close adjacency, the bloom of the sitter even further blanched by the years, and her restricted social agency augmented by physical crippling. This is the widow Mrs. Smith, a minor enough character, but one who increases in prominence the closer Anne's marriage plot comes to fruition—so much so, in fact, that, with the parallel drawn in the novel's last paragraph, she becomes virtually as important as Anne herself: "Her spring of felicity was in the glow of her spirits, as her friend Anne's was in the warmth of her heart" (252). What has come to rescue Mrs. Smith, of course, is not some Captain Wentworth, but her own proto-novelistic love of news, of managing its acquisition and distribution, and most of all, "of telling the whole story her own way" (211) in a world where, as Anne herself has had occasion to note, "men have had every advantage of [women] in telling their own story" (234). The intimate final pairing of widow and bride not only invites us to construe Mrs. Smith as a sort of Anne without a conventional happy ending, but helps keep us envisioning Anne without one, too. For however much the latter glories in being a sailor's wife, "she must pay the tax of quick alarm for belonging to that profession" (252): a reminder, in the novel's concluding sentence, that its heroine might at any moment relapse, on the far side of marriage, into the desolate state of the Unmarried One.

There is no missing the implication of this final diptych in which a near-spinster on one panel is joined to a near-novelist on the other—namely, that if No One *were* ever to incarnate itself, it would be thus bleakly: in a character who is at once as pathetic as the unmarried Anne *has been*, and as desperately upbeat as her ailing, but imaginative alter ego Mrs. Smith *has become*. Of the stylothete who once figured in the novels only as their god, the glorious watchword had been: "Better no representation than a demeaning one"; now, however, it seems in the course of being altered to "Better any representation, no matter how pitiful or sentimental, than none whatsoever." When Elizabeth or Emma bowed to the necessity of a similar reversal, she landed on her feet, on the pillowed turf of successful socialization, but No One, once it fell into personhood, could drop only to unredeemed doom. For in finally yielding to the gravity of the social demand *to characterize itself*, to occupy a subject position whose imprisoning psychosocial coordinates would put her (as we might finally be allowed to say) in her humbled place, No One would both give away the secret of Austen Style, and forgo all the authority it had been able to assume. Having shown itself for the injured utterance of a woman and spinster, it would have simultaneously assented to its social circumscription as such. The feats of transcendence that formerly secured our universal acknowledgment of its knowledge-as-universal could no longer even be imagined.

At the core of the poignancy that readers find so irresistible in *Persuasion* is not Anne's despondency or the equally painful, plainly overcompensating cheerfulness of Mrs. Smith, but our impression that both these things are being proffered—with a delicacy, a discretion, that makes the gesture all the more heartbreaking—as the twin faces of the stylothete's personal agony. The sadness readers feel for the heroine and her double is simply an acceptable way to acknowledge the much less innocuous sadness they feel *for the novel*, for the headlong fall of Austen Style into the personal abasement it had constituted itself against. Elizabeth Bennet spoke an earlier Austen's mind when she declared condolence in misfortune "insufferable" (PP 293). And in truth, our commiseration for the author of *Persuasion* is no freer from schadenfreude than the equally well-contented sorrow people feel on learning of the personal problems of a celebrity, or on observing the wrinkling and thickening of a famous beauty. The thrill of finally getting to feel sorry for an indifferent god who has now fallen homeless to earth is apparently so overwhelming that, by way of managing it, we cannot declare its occasion "moving" too many times. "Moving, affecting, touching, poignant": the inevitable litany of tributes, whatever else it may do, serves to mystify our relief at no longer having to take Austen Style seriously. Under the guise of compassion for the stylothete's incipient slide into personification, we vent our furious resentment against whoever dares imagine standing outside the social conditions that we have resigned ourselves to suffer.

It is depressing to hear the new vulnerability of *Persuasion* hailed as an extended "reach" for the novelist, when in fact it amounts to the retraction of her great world-historical achievement, which is to have established, within the boundlessly oppressive imperiums of gender, conjugality, and the Person, something like extraterritoriality. We have called that extraterritoriality, or rather the audacious presumption of it: (her) Style. If *Emma* refuses to mourn what is given up in Austen Style, *Persuasion* envisions getting it back, somehow or other, cost what it may. And that cost would ultimately encompass the sacrifice of the very ethos of Austen Style, which, as a connoisseurship-based criticism long ago observed, is already faltering here in a narration whose abrupt mood swings weaken its usual confidence, even as its frequent shifts of diction thin out the discursive consistency that was the linguistic badge of such confidence. Critical commonplace to the contrary, *Emma* is a decidedly melancholic book, and *Persuasion* only a very sad one.

III

Persuasion, however, is not Austen's only reflection on the idea and form of the disappearance of Style. The meditation begun there is revisited—and radically revised—in *Sanditon*, the novel satirizing hypochondria that Austen, unfeignedly ill, died before completing. If *Persuasion* had broached the great (and greatly banal) temptation of Austen Style to revert to the Person it had constituted itself against, "The Last Work," as a fitting gravity led Austen's family to denominate *Sanditon*, concludes her oeuvre with a decisive return to form—or at any rate to the self-negation on which that form was founded. Negation had always been the prime mover of Absolute Style, its constant recourse for whatever ailed the author whose (social, psycho-logical, physical) person it voided. No more than we glimpsed the spinster writer in *Emma*, do we espy the dying writer per-sonified among *Sanditon*'s imaginary invalids, whose bogus ail-ments serve merely, faute de mieux, to grab the lion's share of social airtime. If a personal narrator does make a brief, crabby appearance in the text, this merely accentuates the author's re-newed refusal to sit for a full portrait, which, especially now that her formerly blooming looks have turned "black & white & every wrong colour" (L 335), could only give to her social mar-ginality the added emphasis of physical repugnance.

Yet neither can we conceal from ourselves that this particular "return to form" does nothing to prevent *Sanditon* from ef-fecting the general formal ruination of the Austen Novel as we have come to know it. Perhaps the most obvious (if not, as we will see, the most damaged) aspect of this ruination reveals an overall structural problem with the text. Though Austen's nephew claimed of *Sanditon* that, even after a dozen chapters, it was difficult to know "what the course of the story was to be" (M 193), the trouble here is not exactly an *irresolute* plot. On the contrary, in its chief articulations at least, the story appears all too determined to carry on its predecessors' business: escorting a nubile heroine through her encounters with the single men whose suitability and intentions she must assess on her way to the successfully married state. What disorients us in *Sanditon* is not the direction of its story, but the structural dissonance between that story—which always, even here, imposes itself as "the" story in Austen—and the intensive thematic concentration on *morbidity*, a theme which engages us in distinctly un- and even anti-conjugal ways. In Mr. Parker's rising spa resort, where an ideology of "Invalidism" presides over proliferating modalities of "self-doctoring" (MW 418, 388), *Sanditon* anticipates the dominion of our present-day health culture, whose discourses, perceptions, and practices, floated broadly over the social space and sunk deep within the subject, arrogantly take priority over everything else.[36] But besides the novel's construction of morbidity into the material site of an endless and all-important health management, we need to observe its simultaneous *de*construction of morbidity into a drive, the hardly conscious but nonetheless insistent push of all things at this site—including the site itself—toward their undoing. As a mere site, morbidity might have provided a relatively unruffled backcloth for Austen's masterplot, a kind of Bath *au petit pied*. But as a drive, it projects certain ends of its own that are totally incongruous with this plot: disaster and death.

For example: high on a hill called Sanditon, whose very name intimates the feebleness of its foundation, the foolish Mr. Parker raises not merely the proverbial house built on sand, but a whole tract of such. And in case the allusion to Matthew isn't sufficiently clear, the text issues portentous weather warnings to reinforce it: Mrs. Parker recalls that, during the past winter, perched above a blue but windy sea, she and her husband were being "literally rocked in [their] bed" by storms, while the Hilliers, in the Parkers' former home below, "did not seem to feel the Storms last Winter at all" or be "aware of the Wind being anything more than common" (MW 381). Even putting aside the hard fact of this shakiness, the ideal character of Sanditon is vitiated in Mr. Parker's airy-fairy imagination as well:

> Nature had marked it out—had spoken in most intelligible Characters—The finest, purest Sea Breeze on the Coast—acknowledged to be so—Excellent Bathing—fine hard Sand—Deep Water 10 yards from the Shore—no Mud—no Weeds—no slimey rocks—Never was there a place more palpably designed by Nature for the resort of the Invalid. . . .
> (MW 369)

Whether or not Sanditon is fine, pure, hard, intelligible, and above all palpably designed, Mr. Parker's account of it is none of these. Mindlessly drifting from phrase to phrase—going nowhere but in circles of obsession—sentence structure itself abandoned for a paratactic run of noun phrases—never was there a prose more urgently in need of a brisk salt rub. Its slapdash composition, suggestive of possibly shoddy construction in the development itself, finds a far more congenial topic in evoking the rot of Brinshore, Sanditon's rival spa:

> What in the name of Common Sense is to *recommend* Brinshore? —A most insalubrious Air—Roads proverbially detestable—Water Brackish beyond example . . . & as for the Soil—it is so cold & ungrateful that it can hardly be made to yeild a Cabbage. (369)

But it is not just Mr. Parker's language that unconsciously "takes sides" with Brinshore; so, more surprisingly, does his taste. No doubt, when he leaves "the constant Eyesore" of his kitchen garden near Sanditon Village, and "the yearly nuisance of its decaying vegetation," for his house on Sanditon Hill, what he flees is a version of Brinshore, which, though "lying . . . between a stagnant marsh, a bleak Moor & the constant effluvia of a ridge of putrifying sea weed," apparently lies also in Sanditon, like death in Arcadia (380, 369). But he justifies his move by saying, "Who can endure a Cabbage Bed in October?"; and the echo reveals a preference for Brinshore's ungrateful soil after all. Topographically near enough to Sanditon for competition, Brinshore is still closer on the imaginary plane, where it figures the morbid landscape that the model spa is not just fearful, but positively desirous, of becoming.

Too pointedly *sabulous* to be credibly *salubrious,* Sanditon seems connotatively destined, like Mr. Parker's overeager speculation on it, to a great crash, except that either fate would be a calamity whose occurrence the consistent comic ethos of Austen's marriage plot depends on proscribing entirely. Another, related proscription—that no major character may die, and no character whatsoever may die "on stage"—would likewise frustrate any possible development of the large-looming, but abidingly static, theme of hypochondria. For only the antiphrasis of death could unfold the folly of hypochondria: the ultimate irrelevance of our minor or mendacious maladies to the great killer that, despite the fuss we make over them, they don't even have the merit of preparing us for. And only the antiphrasis of death could let us grasp the grain of truth that, in among its salts and vials, hypochondria nonetheless contains: that we are indeed always suffering from something that will be "the death of us"—life.[37] But like disaster, death, as Austen understood in *Emma,* is "news . . . to throw every thing else into the back-ground" (E 387). So while *Sanditon* finds its principal themes, of catastrophe and mortality, in the terrible drive of all things to their doom, its dozen chapters hardly encourage us to wager that these themes will precipitate in significant emplotment. Granted that the novel's engrossing interest in morbidity makes the motions of the marriage plot cursory and almost affectless, its fidelity to this plot keeps that interest, however fertile in incident, from germinating into large-scale narrative realization and resolution. That Sanditon should find itself reduced to rubble, and the Parkers to penury, or that Diana or Susan Parker should act the principal in a deathbed scene—such outcomes become as imaginable, thanks to the insistence of connotation, as they must remain unrealizable, owing to the persistence of the marriage plot. The twentieth-century "Lady" who completed *Sanditon* with the usual quota of couplings, and the equally typical dearth of disasters, understood something fundamental to the narrative of the novel as Austen left it: that its pursuit of the marriage plot would necessarily deprive the morbid drive of a motor.[38] In the end, Sanditon would prove only a somewhat dappled version of *Emma*'s South End, the bathing place where, Isabella reports, "We all had our health perfectly well" and "never found the least inconvenience from the mud" (E 105).

That *Sanditon* is always verging on a collapse that will never take place, however, indicates only a faulty construction; it is nothing, a trivial blemish, compared to the infinitely more involving collapse that does occur: the breakdown, registered on every page of the novel, of Austen Style. It has long been whispered among the Janeites, of course, that *Sanditon* is by no means so well written as the other six novels; and certainly, it is no harder to detect where Austen's hand left off and another Lady's began in the completed *Sanditon*, than it is to discern repeated failures of Absolute Style in Austen's own part. No matter how we eventually come to understand and evaluate these failures, they furnish clear evidence that the morbid drive immobilized plotwise has been internalized by a Style that, in thus defaulting, gives it a kind of fulfillment even so. *Sanditon*'s great discovery: personification is not the only way for Style to default; Style may default no less by very faults of style, by "bad form." For however impersonal the figure of No One has heretofore been, it has always been a figure nonetheless, in the quasi-plastic sense of a unity, an orientation. Now, by an extension of the logic that had determined its originary constitution as No One, this figure comes to embrace its anonymous condition still more radically as . . . nothing at all. In its bad writing, *Sanditon* would dramatize the only death scene to be found in all Austen: the passing of the stylothete.

The better to measure these faults of style in *Sanditon*, it will be convenient if I first indulge a confession. Whenever I write, I fear this more than anything else: *writing badly.* Accordingly, against an imagined charge of "ill written," I diligently produce signs of a will to style, as though in style—not this style or that, but what I imagine as Style itself: linguistic mastery of an absolute kind—lay my only security. Yet in turning out these signs, I can hardly help recognizing them as such; and so I am condemned to be always observing the discrepancy between a mere will to style and Style as an accomplished fact. I consequently fuss—fret—adjust—anguish lest my style, even with its lowercase *s*, die of the shame of uncorrected because unnoticed faults: not so much lapses of grammar as a too often or too closely repeated construction, an inadvertent rhyme or accidental alliteration, a word or phrase that without any knowledge of mine, and contrary to any intention, is noisily insisting on itself, betraying my stupidity in not "catching" it, or even worse, some secret obsession I have not even been aware of trying to hide. And eventually, as anyone not myself could have foretold, I detect, emblazoned in this sentence or that, the scarlet illiteracy of which I have painstakingly tried to divest my prose. Here glares the gross solecism that I have unmistakably committed, or the ludicrous suggestion of the signifier that, without actually heeding it, I have unwittingly taken. The discovery, of course, only impels me to more intense scrutiny, since it is precisely when I have caught such a lapse that I feel the full force of the shame I imagine I would have felt if I hadn't. And, to make matters worse, this ever-necessary watchfulness needs to be constantly watched in turn: certainly, where style is concerned, one can never be careful enough, but it is equally true that, where style is concerned, neither must one be *too* careful, or the desired effect will rigidify into affectation, a "manner" that, like certain muscular spasms, chokes the underlying nerve.

While we will never know whether Jane Austen actually *suffered* from this paranoia of style, we can be perfectly sure that she *shared* it. "Though in composition she was equally rapid and correct," her brother Henry tells us in the Biographical Notice, "yet an invincible distrust of her own judgment induced her to withhold her works from the public, till time and many perusals had satisfied her that the charm of recent composition was dissolved" (NA 4). It isn't hard to guess the avalanche of abashment she imagined might overtake her if, in a hurry, she had omitted these frequent perusals. In *Mansfield Park*, when Fanny Price must write an immediate response to a note from Mary Crawford on Henry's proposal, the narration remarks: "had there been time for scruples and fears as to style, she would have felt them in abundance" (MP 307); and even as it is, "she had no doubt that her note must appear excessively ill-written, that the language would disgrace a child" (308). "How I have blushed over the pages of her writing!" Edward says of Lucy's correspondence in *Sense and Sensibility*, as though, committed by a future wife, her egregious errors must throw shame on him too. The note in which she breaks off with him, he avers, "is the only letter I ever received from her, of which the substance made me any amends for the defect of the style" (SS 365). And though Emma does not find any such disqualifying defect in Robert Martin's proposal to Harriet, that is certainly what, in reading it, she is hoping to pin on him. Over any writer in Austen (even, apparently, a child) hangs the possible humiliation of being defective in style, of being so narcissistically attached to one's prose, or so assured of a maternally benevolent reception of it, that one would fail to see what made it defective. Nor is this potential for mortification by any means suspended when a letter, like Frank Churchill's to his new stepmother, is passed around to general admiration.

> For a few days every morning visit in Highbury included some mention of the handsome letter Mrs. Weston had received. "I suppose you have heard of the handsome letter Mr. Frank Churchill had written to Mrs. Weston? I understand it was a very handsome letter, indeed. . . . Mr. Woodhouse saw the letter, and he says he never saw such a handsome letter in his life." (E 18)

On all of which the narration, as if upholding a higher standard than would permit its assent to even such universal praise, which has become a mere jargon, passes this dryly corrective judgment: "It was, indeed, a highly-prized letter."

The possibility of shame in writing—the shame of falling into language that "would disgrace a child"—naturally engenders the ferocity of a stylistic vigilance that would have already forestalled any such lapse. (Henry Austen boasts that, given a father who was a profound scholar and a man of exquisite taste, "it is not wonderful that his daughter Jane should, at a very early age, have become sensible to the charms of style, and enthusiastic in the cultivation of her own language" [NA 3]. But this is actually the fact most worthy of our wonder: what complex of forces converted a passive "sensibility" to another's style into the enthusiastic cultivation of one's own?)[39] The impulse to put both the world and the word under correction is a powerful one in Austen, much in excess of whatever moral rationale usually accompanies it. Whether the fault in question is a semantic choice, a grammatical usage, a perception, or even a disposition, it must be corrected, or at any rate put into the category, by no means thinly populated in Austen, of "the incorrigible," where correction consists not in removing or punishing the fault, but in endlessly remarking on it.

It's not just that Austen Style tries hard to be correct—few styles do not—but that it obeys an overwhelming urge to give correctness *a theatrical form*. To manifest grammatical correctness as spectacle—that is the point of the point of its epigrams. Even of a nonepigrammatical Austen sentence, try normalizing the typical inversion; correct the sentence would remain, but gone would be the acrobatic somersault that flaunts this correctness, that supplements grammatical completion with artistic finish. Think, too, of the numerous binaries that burrow through *any* Austen sentence, and open this unit of Style to the additional closure of matched-up opposites (in *the* sentence, for instance: universal/single; man/wife; possession/want). Or think of the famous adjectival triads that boast the power of Style to mount a Person with no more than three pins, and all as elegant, exact, and final, as Emma Woodhouse is handsome, clever, and rich.[40] Such articulations do more than organize a sentence; they *overorganize* it, as if Style were secretly prey to a fear of losing itself in a linguistic fluidity that endangered the very possibility of controlling it.

As Chapman notes, and we can see for ourselves in the published facsimile, the unfinished manuscript of *Sanditon*—the last child, as we might put it, of Austen's shame—"contains a very large number of erasures and interlineations" (FN, Preface). With the exception of *The Watsons*, also unfinished, and the canceled chapter of *Persuasion*, this is the only manuscript that survives of an Austen novel; and though we know that Austen also revised her other novels, the actual sight of her revisions is nonetheless as disturbing as if, at the bottom of a vase filled with beautifully arranged flowers, we had caught a glimpse of thin filigrees of blood where the stems had been cut.

For the most part, these corrections are neither consequential nor revealing: "period" replaces "time," and "blunders" "mistakes"; "the next morning" becomes "all the following morning," and the like. But there is one correction, more curious than the rest, that demands attention here. At almost the very end of the manuscript as illness obliged her to leave it, Austen originally described the park paling around Lady Denham's estate as having "vigorous Elms, or old Thorns and Hollies following its line almost every where" (FN, notes to 167). But she later emended the phrase so that it read, "clusters of fine Elms, or rows of old Thorns following its line almost every where" (MW 426). Where, we can't but wonder, have all the hollies gone—the very species of tree that had at first received most emphasis, not only of course from its terminal position in the list of trees, but also from the dactylic pressure that the first part of the doubleted phrase brought to bear on the second ("vígorous Élms, or / óld Thorns and Hóllies")? Have they vanished, as we might be at first inclined to suppose, for some banal botanical reason? During the composition of *Mansfield Park*, Austen famously asked her sister Cassandra if she "could discover whether Northamptonshire is a Country of Hedgerows" (L 202), to check the reference she had just made to them; and after the publication of *Emma*, her brother Henry pointed out an error that similiar inquiry would have spared her: "Jane, I wish you would tell me where you get those apple-trees of yours that come into bloom in July."[41] But in fact investigation shows the holly to be quite within its range along the English coast where *Sanditon* is set. Alternatively, we might speculate that the revision was introduced, as revisions often are, by the author's sense of having repeated herself. In *Persuasion*, which immediately preceded *Sanditon*, Anne Elliot, protected by "a bush of low rambling holly," had overheard a conversation between Louisa and Captain Wentworth (P 88); and here, through a gap in the arboreal lining of the fence, Charlotte is allowed, equally by accident, to spy on Miss Brereton and Sir Edward. But there is a far more conspicuous repetition of which, without having to leave Sanditon, we are reminded a page later. For if Lady Denham acquired her title from her second husband, Sir Harry, whose portrait is given pride of place over the mantelpiece in the sitting room, she got her property, this property as a matter of fact, from her first husband, Mr. Hollis, whom "one among many Miniatures in another part of the room, little conspicuous, represented." "Poor Mr. Hollis!" thinks Charlotte in the last sentence of the manuscript. "It was impossible not to feel him hardly used; to be obliged to stand back in his own House & see the best place by the fire constantly occupied by Sir H. D." (MW 427). Might not the hollies, then, have gone to eliminate the possibility of noticing this non-elective affinity of signifiers: Mr. Hollis' hollies? Austen had mocked such stupid, automatic affinities as early as "Love and Friendship," where a character named Sophia is allowed to sigh and faint upon the Sofa (88) and is later distressed by "the azure [of a sky] varied by … delicate streaks of white" because it reminds her of her lost husband's "blue sattin Waistcoat," also "striped with white!" (98). On a couple of rare occasions, Austen had herself fallen victim to such inadvertent and (as soon as they are noticed) ridiculous affinities: when, for instance, she has a character named Mr. Palmer say to his wife, "don't palm all your abuses of language upon me" (SS 113); or when, during their visit to Pemberley, the Gardiners are "consigned over to the gardener" (PP 251); or when, in a letter, Austen mentions, sans irony, that "Tom Chute has had a fall from his horse" (L 106).

So free, so undisciplined an associationism of the signifier can hardly be tolerated, much less indulged, by the realism of the Austen Novel, where as in the examples just given, it ludicrously flattens the imaginary depth of representation into the literal surface of a linguistic performance. Nor, for a separate but concomitant reason, can it be taken very far by Austen Style, which, parading its command of language in every sentence, cannot afford many such signs of having spun out of control. Before everybody in Meryton declares Wickham "the wickedest young man in the world" (PP 294), the novel has had three hundred pages to keep the association at bay, and even then it is given as the work of townspeople who, in their ignorance of just how bad Wickham has been, seem all the more unconsciously enslaved to alliteration. Ultimately, then, what Austen aims to eradicate with the hollies is *any* evidence of this irrational dreamwork of the signifier. I have no way of proving my contention, except by appeal to what I take to be a general experience of the paranoia of style that Austen seems to have felt with peculiarly creative intensity. But to make the case, if not more persuasive to those who have never experienced this paranoia, more coherent to those who have, let me proceed to examine, at the beginning of *Sanditon*, an uncorrected case of a phenomenon similar to "Mr. Hollis' hollies." The carriage conveying Mr. and Mrs. Parker has overturned, and within hardly more than a dozen lines of text, we are told (1) that they notice "a Cottage . . . romantically situated among *wood* on a high Eminence at some little Distance"; (2) that their accident has itself been "discerned from a *Hay*field adjoining the House they had passed"; and (3) that the "well-looking *Hale*, Gentlemanlike Man, of middle age, the Proprietor of the Place, who happened to be among his *Hay*makers at the time" is a Mr. *Heywood*, father to our heroine Charlotte (MW 364–65; emphasis added). It is as though Emma had been introduced coming out of a log cabin, or Elinor sprinting through a grove. The effect would be comic in Dickens (or in Beckett, who may have had it in mind when he wrote that Austen had "much to teach" him); it is comic in Austen, too, but in a way so little consonant with the overall realism of her fiction, and so very refractory to the discipline of her verbal minimalism, that we can hardly decide whether she is deliberating a departure, or just surrendering to a drift, from both the Novel and the Style this Novel has served so well.[42]

Even in *Sanditon*, of course, many such repetitions of the signifier, ruled by the conscious principle of wit, are classically meaningful: "Apply any Verses you like to [Brinshore]," Mr. Heywood tells the injured Mr. Parker, "But I want to see something applied to your Leg" (370). Moreover, it is often a character who is responsible for displaying the signifier's unconscious determinism. Lady Denham, for instance, says of the school of girls expected at Sanditon: "Who knows but some may be consumptive & want Asses milk—& I have two Milch asses at this present time.—But perhaps the little Misses may hurt the Furniture" (393). If the asses' milk, first turned to milch asses, finally condenses into little Misses, only her ladyship's obsessive meanness is to blame. Similarly, the poet Burns "is always on fire" and "all ardour" only in Sir Edward's inflamed imagination (397, 398). But the majority of such patterns emerge, independent of character, under the aegis of pure narration. No less oddly than Mr. Heywood enters our vision amidst hay and wood, the Hilliers are said to reside (as some of my readers will already have observed) at the *bottom* of Sanditon Hill. In another instance, the same sentence that calls Lady Denham's figure "upright" terms her manner "downright"; though no semantic contradiction prevents the sentence from making sense, neither does any clear sign of intended wordplay do away with our sense that the first word has stupidly triggered the choice of the second (391). And likewise, when in the small scope of two succeeding clauses, the description of Sanditon Village moves from cottages "smartened up with a white Curtain & 'Lodgings to Let' " to "two Females in elegant white . . . with their books & camp stools" (383), the two whites, by no means identically shaded, clash in a way that seems more negligent than deliberate. As Austen Style goes, they are neither properly separated, so as to protect genteel elegance from appearing soiled from the start with the residue of vulgar smartening, nor properly conjoined, say, by an observation that would turn their very intimacy into a telling irony. The tangle, slight in itself, is soon compounded by the introduction of a Mrs. Whitby and a Miss Whitby, who run a library cum trinket shop (389–90); and by the time Charlotte glimpses "something White & Womanish" over what the narration has just called "the *pales*" (426, emphasis added), the ramifying insistence of the "white" signifier has grown positively nonsensical, as if in her maturity Austen were beginning, without acknowledging it, perhaps without even knowing it, a second collection of juvenilia. The extirpation of the hollies, then, would amount to no more than a token gesture of resistance to a process that runs rampant throughout *Sanditon*: the undoing of Style by a wordplay whose problematic governance places this text, uniquely in its author's oeuvre, beyond the reach of correction.

As we've already begun to see, much of this undecidable wordplay, this Anti-Style, turns on the letter H, object here of a veritable fetish: besides Mr. and Mrs. Heywood and their fourteen children, of whom one is Miss H., the heroine, there is Reverend Mr. Hanking, visitor to Sanditon; William Heeley, shoemaker at Sanditon; Thomas Hillier, tenant of Mr. Parker's former home in Sanditon Village; and of course Mr. Hollis, late of the hollies at Sanditon House. Mr. Parker intends to "proceed to Hailsham, & so Home ... home, from Hailsham" (367), where the only important thing about the directions is the chiasmus of H words that they permit. It is much the same with those merely named, otherwise undescribed, unvisited, or even unbuilt Sanditon locales: House, Hotel, and Hospital. But the most obsessively repeated H word in the text is surely *hill*, as in, preeminently, the hill on which modern Sanditon is built. In the course of only a couple of pages, we read "one other Hill brings us to Sanditon," "at first it is Uphill work," "they were now approaching ... the foot of the Hill they were afterwards to ascend," "if the *Village* could attract, the Hill might be nearly full," "now, for our Hill, our health-breathing Hill" (380–83). What Barthes calls "the goddess H." beckons with the pleasure potential of homosexuality and hashish;[43] no less euphoric, Austen's aspirate presides over the hale, the healing, and the whole—or would, that is, if the unfortunate phrase "our health-breathing Hill" did not breathe health too heavily not to give the game away. So densely distributed as to convey, by onomatopoeia, the whole hard labor of respiration, the aspirate comes virtually to stand on its own, detached from, most strikingly, one phoneme in particular: *ill*. And once *h/ill* is thus split apart in our minds, two equally unlovely prospects open before us. In the one direction, that phoneme becomes suddenly visible all over the place, as if finally enabled to peep out from what had been countless other hiding spots: on the Bills at the Window, in the Milliner's Shop, the Billiard Room, and the unfinished Buildings. We may now detect its earlier insistence in the two Willingdens and Sanditon Village, and are attuned to recognize its later recurrence in the heroine's reference to *Camilla* and in other characters' condition of being "bilious" or "ill-used." And in the other direction, the letter H, failing to do its work by *overdoing* it, seems no less absented than if it had been dropped by a vulgar country or cockney pronunciation, or—threat of a considerably broader *déclassement*—stopped by a momentary loss of breath.[44] Sanditon's "health-breathing Hill" breaks Austen's H-ing art in pieces—quite literally—and there is no mending it.

Is this what happens to No One when the author who has projected that figure knows she is about to assume the even more radical form of nonbeing that is death? Or better, is this how the stylothete anticipates the author's fate in the very exercise of Style, so that the Work would reach its end in advance of the Life—a Life whose sibylline last words, "I want nothing but Death" (NA 5), might then seem to be no more than the logical inference from the Work? Previously in Austen, what we were given instead of the Person had always been the dazzling spectacle of Style, which produced on us the impression of utter perfection, of a "pen" from which, as Henry Austen put it, "every thing came finished," and on all subjects ideas were as clear as expressions were well chosen (NA 8). But here, in the thematic vicinity of what roadsigns will no doubt soon be calling Sanditon-Brinshore, what we mainly see is Austen Style decomposing into a mixture that is, like the upsetting soil of Sanditon's first hill, "half rock, half sand" (MW 364). The granite of the Sentence crumbles before our incredulous eyes into a grit of sounds, senses, letters, that scatter themselves across the text into patterns that seem neither entirely intentional, nor entirely random. No less than one of Austen's own heroines, Style is "humbled to the dust" (NA 173).

This dust, however, is not the mortal clay of the Person, but the livelier quicksand of language, and it is to language and not the Person that Austen Style—writerly even in extremis— ultimately surrenders its claims to mastery. Before, the object of mourning in the Austen Novel had been a foregone personhood; now, what is to be mourned is the Style that used to stand in place of that personhood—or rather, by an almost unthinkably austere logic of neither/nor, what is to be mourned is both the one *and* the other. *Emma* allowed us to envision the utopia of a double perfection, the perfection of Style matched to that of Person; *Sanditon* reaches toward the perhaps more feasible state of their double, their simultaneous annihilation. If the letter H works in this novel-fragment as a sign of the negation that founds Austen Style (h/ill), it is also, by means of the highly improper, even silly wordplay generated around it, a sign of the negation of this negation, Style's literal last gasp before it becomes, shall I say, with feelings badly conflicted, that ill writing in which *all* writing eventually recognizes itself. "She wrote whilst she could hold a pen, and with a pencil when a pen was become too laborious" (NA 4).

Afterimage

Untitled ("House-Tree-Person Technique" by John N. Buck)
Robert Beck 2000, graphite and charcoal, 12" x 9"

Notes

This essay evolved from the Mrs. William Beckman Lectures, which its author gave at the University of California, Berkeley, in 2000. He is glad to gather around him, if only nominally, the collaborators whom he couldn't do without: Robert Beck, Leo Bersani, Carol Christ, Nicholas Dames, Lee Edelman, Adam Feldman, Philip Fisher, Catherine Gallagher, Amanpal Garcha, Steven Ho, David Kurnick, Joseph Litvak, Franco Moretti, Ida Miller, Laura Mullen, Mary Murrell, Kent Puckett, Elaine Scarry, Hilary Schor, and Alex Woloch. Great friend to Austen and the author alike, Mary Ann O'Farrell must bear with finding her name curtailed in the phrase: for M. A.

1. Jane Austen, *Emma*, in *The Novels of Jane Austen*, ed. R. W. Chapman, 5 vols. (London: Oxford University Press, 1932–34), 4: 76. I have used Chapman's edition for all the novels, as well as his editions of the *Minor Works* (London: Oxford University Press, 1954); the *Letters*, 3d edition, expanded and reannotated by Deirdre Le Faye (Oxford: Oxford University Press, 1995); and James Edward Austen-Leigh's *Memoir of Jane Austen* [2d edition, 1871] (Oxford: Clarendon Press, 1927). For convenience, *Sanditon* is quoted from the *Minor Works*, except for Austen's corrections to the manuscript; there I fol-

low the notes given in Chapman's first published edition of the text, *Fragment of a Novel* (Oxford: Clarendon Press, 1925). Hereafter, citations will appear parenthetically in the text according to the following scheme of abbreviation:

Sense and Sensibility = SS
Pride and Prejudice = PP
Mansfield Park = MP
Emma = E
Northanger Abbey = NA
Persuasion = P
Minor Works = MW
Fragment of a Novel = FN
Letters = L
Memoir of Jane Austen = M

A page number with no accompanying letter should be taken to indicate the last work specified.

2. Throughout this essay, I have capitalized Style where it suggests absolute impersonality; where it appertains to an obvious personal project, I have kept it in lowercase. But as will be shown, Austen's "Style" is tangent to the "style" of her characters on so many planes that my practice of this principle never quite makes it perfect.

3. "And then, what do you think we did? We dressed up Chamberlayne in woman's clothes, on purpose to pass for a lady,—only think what fun! Not a soul knew of it, but Col. and Mrs. Forster, and Kitty and me, except my aunt, for we were forced to borrow one of her gowns; and you cannot imagine how well he looked! When Denny, and Wickham, and Pratt, and two or three more of the men came in, they did not know him in the least. Lord! how I laughed! and so did Mrs. Forster. I thought I should have died" (PP 221). And Chamberlayne—did he think so too?

4. Leo Bersani, "Is the Rectum a Grave?" *October* 43 (1987): 208. To the author of this lacerating passage, I owe the shaping opportunity to talk through much of the present essay; over more than one crux, I hitchhiked a ride on his large, fast intelligence. Whence, then, as my readers will shortly see, the irresistible ingratitude of my desire to respond to the passage *in kind?* All I know is that, if Bersani has only once been an *Austen* critic (in the *Mansfield Park* chapter of *A Future for Astyanax* [Boston: Little, Brown, 1976]), he remains in all his works, by virtue of their practice and understanding of style, our most *Austenian.*

5. For does anyone suppose that the trick aborts, and the two men shake hands and part, once this mutual éclaircissement has taken place? Wouldn't this be, on the contrary, the moment at which the sex—the distinctively *gay* sex—usually begins? Certainly, in any event, now is when it begins to get interesting.

6. Roland Barthes, *Mythologies*, tr. Annette Lavers (New York: Hill and Wang, 1972), p. 125; and Roland Barthes, *Mythologies* [1957], in *Oeuvres complètes*, ed. Eric Marty, 3 vols. (Paris: Seuil, 1993), 1: 695 ("une parole figée . . . se suspend, tourne sur elle-même et rattrape une généralité"). All subsequent citations from works by Barthes will also provide his French text from this edition, hereafter identified as *OC*. I make this link between the mass-cultural interpellation of Barthesian Myth and the cult-making imperative of Austen Style to suggest a sense in which, structurally, the two aren't all that far apart. Both impose on their respective publics the phenomenon of a peremptory language that can only be refused at the price of extreme isolation (whether by dropping out of common culture in the case of Myth, or out of whatever counts as cultivation in the case of Style) and can only be accepted through a slavish identification with its source of emission. Refusal would seem to entail so severe a solitude, and acceptance so drastic a docility, as to abolish selfhood as we usually know it in either case. From the standpoint of the *power* each

structure commands, however, Myth and Style stand exactly a world apart. For it is as a universal discourse that Myth remains forever exempt from the charges of elitism that it is consequently enabled to rain, like so many blows, on Style as the work of a single individual. This ritual censuring of Style's exclusiveness lays a convenient embargo on contemplating the inclusiveness, Myth's own, from which there is no escape.

7. Marcel Proust, *Contre Sainte-Beuve* (Paris: Gallimard, 1954), p. 257, my translation.

8. Virginia Woolf, "Jane Austen at Sixty," *Athenaeum*, December 15, 1923 and *New Republic*, January 30, 1924; reprinted in *Jane Austen: The Critical Heritage*, ed. B. C. Southam, 2 vols. (London: Routledge and Kegan Paul, 1968, 1987), 2: 301. It should be noted that Woolf dropped this sarcasm in revising her essay for *The Common Reader*. One can only regret the excision, by virtue of which Woolf rendered herself not just a more civil writer—the canon, apparently, was not to be kept waiting—but also, in the worst sense, a more common reader, content like every other to leave this audacious cultural observation (audacious for saying what everyone in fact silently believes) where it usually lies: in the discreet realm, at once titillating and trivialized, of the Open Secret. The regular retreat to this realm whenever homosexuality is concerned seems also to explain why Southam, whose painstaking scholarship has provided us with our only non-archival access to early Jane Austen criticism, strangely splits his excerpt from the *Athenaeum* article into two, so that the Viriginia Woolf who gets named in his table of contents is remarkable only for considering Austen "the forerunner of Henry James and of Proust," while the Virgina Woolf capable of nastily observing the gay-male valence of Austen's work is anonymous there, her observation having been exiled to a catch-all compilation of "some minor highlights of the Jane Austen literature" called merely "Miscellanea: 1871–1938."

9. Frances Ferguson, "*Emma* and the Impact of Form," *MLQ*, March 2000, p. 173.

10. Franco Moretti, *Atlas of the European Novel: 1800–1900* (London and New York: Verso, 1998), p. 18.

11. Roland Barthes, *Writing Degree Zero,* tr. Annette Lavers and Colin Smith (New York: Hill and Wang, 1968), p. 10; and *Le Degré zéro de l'écriture* [1953], in *OC,* 1: 146 ("Quel que soit son raffinement, le style a toujours quelque chose de brut"). Barthes, of course, has no interest in developing this interesting point: he only somatizes style in order to privatize it, to close it to social signification as a secret and a solitude. See also, therefore, Joseph Litvak, *Strange Gourmets: Sophistication, Theory, and the Novel* (Durham, N.C.: Duke University Press, 1997), which, while focusing on what Barthes calls the "carnal structure" of style (as found, par excellence, in the matter of *taste*), demonstrates how this structure is elaborated in, and only in, the modes of the body's social disciplining.

12. Letter to Sir William Elford, April 3, 1815, in *The Life of Mary Russell Mitford, related in a selection from her letters to her friends,* ed. Reverend A. G. L'Estrange, 2 vols. (London, 1870), 1: 306.

13. And even this defense, like the others that have followed in its footsteps, submits to the pull of the trope it would dismiss: "A work of art may be perfect technically and yet be a minor work, a porcelain vase, an ormolu snuff-box. And Jane Austen, though she is not one of the imperial monarchs of fiction, is still less a manufacturer of snuff-boxes" (Lord David Cecil, *Jane Austen* [Cambridge: Cambridge University Press, 1935], pp. 22–23). Austen's technically perfect works are not minor, do not have the status of snuff boxes; yet if neither are they major, the yield of one of fiction's imperial monarchs, then how far can they plausibly be said to transcend that status?

14. For my understanding of how these mutual exclusions determine the first sentence of *Pride and Prejudice,* see D. A. Miller, "Austen's Attitude," *Yale Journal of Criticism* 8, no. 1 (1995): 1–5.

15. The implied distinction here between "the question *who is the character whose point of view orients the narrative perspective?* and the very different question *who is the narrator?*—or, more simply, the

question *who sees?* and the question *who speaks?*" comes from Gérard Genette, *Narrative Discourse* [*Figures III* (Paris: Seuil, 1972)], tr. Jane E. Lewin (Ithaca: Cornell University Press, 1980), p. 186.

16. "Neutral" accents have their social coordinates too, of course, but, at least until other "non-neutral" accents have achieved a certain social power of their own, the former pass unrecognized, confused with the general consciousness for which they are thereby entitled to speak. Written at a later historical moment, Austen's narration might have been forced to declare its authority as "bourgeois," and at a still later one, as "white"; but for now such specifications are largely invisible in the presumption, shared by author and readers, of their generality.

17. For other evidence of how precious anonymity was to Austen, see R. W. Chapman, *Jane Austen: Facts and Problems* (Oxford: Clarendon Press, 1949), pp. 130–39.

18. I take these phrases from two successive fragments entitled "Le neutre—the neutral" and "Actif/passif—active/passive" in Roland Barthes, *Roland Barthes by Roland Barthes*, tr. Richard Howard (New York: Noonday, 1977), pp. 132–33; and *Roland Barthes par Roland Barthes* [1975], in *OC*, 3: 196–97 ("l'insignifiance délectable," "la vacance de 'la personne,' " "l'absence de l'imago," "la discrétion," "le principe de délicatesse," "une sexualité heureuse"). As everywhere in Barthes from *S/Z* on, the usage of *le neutre* here turns on a sexual-grammatical ambiguity which makes it an apt term for at once articulating male homosexuality and closeting the articulation in structural generality. This ambiguity, along with the issue that has required it, virtually disappears when the term is rendered as "the neutral," a sedation which works, precisely, to neutralize the sexually active meaning of Barthes's French. For a similar erasure, compare the published English translation of the first sentence of *Writing Degree Zero*. Barthes had written: "Hébert ne commençait jamais un numéro du *Père Duchêne* sans y mettre quelques 'foutre' et quelques 'bougre' " (*OC*, 1: 139); or, as it is no great stretch to render in English, "Hébert

never began an issue of *Père Duchêne* without throwing in a few *fucks* and *buggers.*" Barthes's translators, however, have metabolized the *foutres* and *bougres* into "a sprinkling of obscenities" (*Writing Degree Zero*, p. 1); and what should have been visible as the weird sophistication of Barthes's repeat performance of these swearwords (whose former power to effect sex intimidation made them precious weapons of the Terror) vanishes into a mystifying euphemism. How Barthes's curious opening sentence bears on his own style, I pursue in "Foutre! Bougre! Ecriture!" *Yale Journal of Criticism* 14, no. 2 (2001): 503–11.

19. Balzac, "Sarrasine," in Roland Barthes, *S/Z*, tr. Richard Miller (New York: Noonday, 1974), p. 229; and *S/Z* [1970], in *OC*, 2: 710 ("forme sans substance").

20. Though, as any reader of *Emma* knows, the word "creature" is attached to many other characters in the novel, it pretty much always bestows this same connotation of sexlessness on whoever is so called. Mrs. Elton's use of it for her "old beau" Mr. Woodhouse is a case in point (302); and even when Mrs. Weston uses it of Emma—"with all dear Emma's little faults, she is an excellent creature" (39)—she is maternally reducing Emma to the child she once had care of, and whom she has been remembering with Mr. Knightley.

21. Mitford, 1: 306.

22. Austen in a letter to her sister Cassandra: "The work is rather too light & bright & sparkling;—it wants shade;—it wants to be stretched out here and there with a long Chapter—of sense if it could be had, if not of solemn specious nonsense—about something unconnected with the story; an essay on Writing, a critique on Walter Scott, or the history of Buonaparte—or anything that would form a contrast and bring the reader with increased delight to the playfulness & Epigrammatism of the general stile" (L 203). Litvak has argued that, by expressing Austen's disapprobation of her own stylistic consistency, this famous passage points up the terroristic nature of her aesthetic of distinction, in which "anything, even an unrelieved 'playfulness and epigrammatism' can fall under the dreaded rubric of the

disgusting" (*Strange Gourmets*, pp. 21–22). This reading, itself quite sparkling, has the merit of alerting us to the paranoia hanging over the practice of Style in Austen, which I'll be pursuing in chapter 3. Yet from the absurdity of "shade" as Austen envisions it here, I incline to think that she is only pretending to regret her novel's consistency and is secretly pleased to be pointing it out. At the beginning of the letter, what she calls her "fits of disgust" appear to owe their origin less to her novel, than—shades of Elizabeth Bennet!—to her mother's "too rapid way" of reading it at an evening party; and the continuation of the passage makes clear that Austen is speaking to be contradicted: "I doubt your quite agreeing with me here—I know your starched Notions." (For a comparably coy antiphrasis, recall: "I am going to take a heroine"—Emma Woodhouse—"whom no one but myself will much like" [M 157; see also p. 60 above].) In any case, supposing Austen *had* endeavored to give her novel shade (in more rational ways, of course, than those she mocks), do we imagine that the chiaroscuro would actually produce the effects she claims? The common reading experience of *Mansfield Park*, the checkered successor to *Pride and Prejudice*, strongly suggests not: the more Fanny, Edmund, or the narrative voice sounds the note of "sense," the less in fact do Mary Crawford's "playfulness and Epigrammatism" delight us when we return to them. More important: even at its most umbrageously moralizing, the prose of the later novel never mounts the smallest test to the overall consistency of Austen's "general stile." Playful or serious, her writing remains pointed, impersonal, elegant, authoritative, and altogether regular in its lexicon, syntax, and rhythms. None of these features is likely to change on account of Napoleon or Walter Scott; and indeed, to put the point more strongly, if Austen Style did treat such subjects, they would probably no longer look "unconnected with the story," since the extreme isotopy of this Style keeps the narrative too from ever seeming to ramble. In a word, Austen here is quite consciously—and correctly—recognizing her work as an extraordinary double departure in the formal history of the novel: a style without inconsistencies, issuing in a narrative without digressions.

23. See Slavoj Žižek on Schelling in *The Abyss of Freedom/Ages of the World* (Ann Arbor: University of Michigan, 1997), p. 7.

24. Thanks to this confusion, or conflation, it follows that Elizabeth feels "most cruelly mortified" by what her father says of Darcy's indifference; "never had [her father's] wit been directed in a manner so little agreeable to her." Although she knows better than her father, of course, and even wonders at his "want of penetration," yet part of her believes him anyway, as if Mr. Bennet's witty obtuseness were proof of his own indifference to her, and must therefore confirm Darcy's; "instead of [Mr. Bennet's] seeing *too little*, she might have fancied *too much*." Characteristically, she continues performing as the favorite: "I am excessively diverted" (PP 363–64).

25. Mr. Bennet to Elizabeth: "I know your disposition, Lizzy. I know that you could be neither happy nor respectable, unless you truly esteemed your husband; unless you looked up to him as a superior. Your lively talents would place you in the greatest danger in an unequal marriage" (376).

26. Though once again, as with all the feats of detachment on display in Austen Style, this one may be telling more than it means to. For if the story in which Elizabeth *falls out* of Austen Style is not a genealogy for the latter, then might it not still be that genealogy *when told backwards?*

27. For it hasn't been by way of its general meaning, as a departure from the universal, from its comfort and its camouflage, that particularity has worked up the largest anxiety in Austen's courtship plots, or has contributed most to dramatic incident. In a more restricted, but more prominent usage (which seems to have died with Austen, the *OED*'s last example of it being E 441), "particularity" also signifies those marked attentions paid to one person by another, as the sign

of amorous interest, of a putative intention to form the Couple. See, for examples, SS 86; MP 316, 362; and E 441. Of this sign, the heroines are, like Fanny, or ought to be, like Marianne, extremely wary, since it is always caught in an ambiguity between meaning and truth that only what Austen calls "a positive engagement" can abolish. Till then, the heroine must always be risking the humiliation of public exposure: of openly responding to a love interest that may not truly exist, or of announcing one of her own that does not prove reciprocal. Austen herself, "dancing and sitting down together" with Tom Lefroy at a series of balls, facetiously claims to have given the company inapt lessons in "how to be particular," her self-mockery forestalling or alleviating the ignominy that would otherwise befall an exhibition that led nowhere: "I can expose myself . . . only once more, because he leaves the country soon" (L 1). The great privilege of Austen's engaged couples, indulged at length in their final retrospections, is precisely this: that they are free at last to expose themselves, to be particular with impunity, since whatever might have been, vaguely or acutely, really or potentially, embarrassing about such particularity before now disappears into the universal social form of the marriage that shelters it.

28. Ferguson, p. 159.

29. Park Honan, *Jane Austen: Her Life* (New York: Faucett Columbine, 1987), p. 72.

30. Honan points out that "Mr. Weston's joking allusion is to the eighteenth-century philosopher of happiness, Francis Hutcheson, who in his *Beauty and Virtue* had worked out a small, bizarre formula with M and A as its keys: 'Since then *Benevolence*, or *Virtue* in any *Agent*,' he had written with some mathematics to help him, 'is as M/A, or M + 1/A, and no *Being* can act above his *natural Ability*; that must be the Perfection of Virtue where M = A, or when the *Being* acts to the utmost of his power for the *publick Good*' " (p. 356).

31. Of course, the narrator of *Mansfield Park*—on one of those rare moments when the narration becomes a narrator—may speak of "my Fanny," as does Jane Austen of "my Emma," when referring either to the novel or the character in her correspondence.

32. Elaine Scarry, *On Beauty and Being Just* (Princeton: Princeton University Press, 1999).

33. Ann Banfield, *Unspeakable Sentences: Narration and Representation in the Language of Fiction* (Boston: Routledge and Kegan Paul, 1982), p. 217. My understanding of the two Emma-could-not-forgive-hers follows on Banfield's distinction between "pure narration" and "represented consciousness."

34. Out of her own cleverness, however, Muriel Spark draws a unique instance of such divination in *The Comforters* [1957] (New York: New Directions, 1994). Here the heroine Caroline suffers a series of apparent hallucinations in which mysterious typing noises usher in a mocking chorus that, speaking "like one person . . . in several tones at once" (54), narrates what she has just thought, said, or done. "It uses a typewriter," she explains. "It uses the past tense. It's exactly as if someone were watching me closely, able to read my thoughts; it's as if the person was waiting to pounce on some insignificant thought or action, in order to make it signify in a strange distorted way" (62). What reader can gainsay her when she becomes convinced that she is a character in a novel being written "on another plane of existence" (63)? As Spark's novel ends, Caroline has herself begun to write a novel, which, it is suggested, may well be—if again "on another plane of existence"—the same one we have just finished reading.

35. David Kurnick, "Throwing Her Voice: *Persuasion*'s Erotics of Indirection." This essay is not yet published, and until it is, I must note that its complex argument is by no means reducible to the part of it I appropriate here.

36. I have more amply discussed this culture in "The Late Jane Austen," *Raritan*, Summer 1990, pp. 55–79. That essay ended with

the sentence, "*Here the manuscript breaks off*," which I meant to identify my text with the unfinished *Sanditon*. I also meant it to register
a certain impasse in my thinking, which didn't yet have a way of
talking about the default of Austen Style in *Sanditon*.

37. *Emma* makes both points on the decease of the hypochondriac
Mrs. Churchill: "A sudden seizure of a different nature from any thing
foreboded by her general state, had carried her off after a short strug-
gle" (E 387). But see also Seneca, Epistle to Lucilius LXXVIII: "Mo-
rieris, non quia aegrotas, sed quia vivis" (you will die, not because
you are sick, but because you are alive).

38. Jane Austen and Another Lady [Anne Telscombe], *Sanditon:
Jane Austen's Last Completed Novel* (Boston: Houghton Mifflin, 1975).

39. Though the present essay has obviously not been written to
answer this question, it does harbor an implicit ambition to stimulate
biography to do so. The numerous Austen lives that have appeared
recently, though all competing fiercely for novelty in reshuffling the
same meager archivia, continue to deny us a psychogenesis of Austen
Style; and even in an age disposed to the bio-novel, we still await
the due account of Austen's curious self-fashioning into the selfless
medium of Style. Yet the alienation of style from self is already pro-
claimed, with the full violence of a conversion, in the juvenilia, which
begin as early as their author's eleventh year. These texts display just
how intensely the young Jane Austen must have felt the oddness of
her fit with grown-up linguistic and literary convention, which she
seems unable to imagine integrating into personal experience. And,
along with this *lived* contradiction, they also signal a *literary* project
for resolving it, for transposing it, at any rate, into a kind of wit that
depends precisely on the bad match between a "style"—say, the jargon of romance—and the mundane-to-absurd situation that the style
is supposed to express. Often enough, moreover, the adult words,
turns, tones, and attitudes that the pubescent Austen incorporates
without assimilating are not just beyond her years, but also—to a
probably catalytic degree—*in the wrong gender*. I have just cited James

Austen's claim that his sister's enthusiastic cultivation of style depended on the (verbal, literary) appeal of the scholar and gentleman who was their father. But the founding editor of the neo-Johnsonian *Loiterer* is surely being too modest; he too, as his own son tells us, "was well read in English literature, had a correct taste, and wrote readily and happily, both in prose and verse"; and he too had "a large share in directing [Jane's] reading and forming her taste" (M 12). Would Austen's famous sangfroid have derived from harnessing the overwhelming enigmatic excitements that the adult male Word was inducing in her, to the work of pretending she was utterly unfazed by them? "Not a puncture, not a weak spot any where" (P 88).

40. At one moment in *Pride and Prejudice*, the superiority of the stylothete over the stylist who aspires to become her is established precisely in terms of Elizabeth's inability to reproduce just such a closure of triangulated terms. So long as the narration has charge of expressing Elizabeth's thoughts, her two youngest sisters are "ignorant, idle, and vain" (PP 213); but as soon as Elizabeth has to put these thoughts before her father in words of her own, Kitty and Lydia become "vain, ignorant, idle, and absolutely uncontrouled!" (231). The "uncontrol," in other words, is also Elizabeth's.

41. Honan, p. 378.

42. There is, of course, another reason why the play of signifiers, that long venerable discovery of Deconstruction, remains so strange, even shocking a phenomenon when sighted in Austen. For the past three decades, Austen scholarship has concentrated on producing one after another study of her referents. Just as naive amateurs once gave their interest in Austen the form of the coaches, gowns, and vicarage houses that illustrate the Chapman edition, so critical professionals now attach their own to the French Revolution, the country estate, and colonial slaving. With its stress on the conjugal imperative and the old maid, my own account of Austen is hardly proposing we ignore the impact of cultural forces and forms on her work; it does, however, stand in implicit polemic with a historicist tradition of un-

derstanding Austen that is indifferent to what most needs to be understood: the originality of her literary achievement as such.

43. Barthes, *Roland Barthes by Roland Barthes*, p. 63; and *Roland Barthes par Roland Barthes*, in *OC*, 3: 143. Despite this passage, it must still be regretted that the general index of Barthes's *Oeuvres complètes*, more faithful than Barthes himself to the closet where he spent most of his life, lacks an entry for *homosexualité*.

44. There are several ways to inform oneself about the social distribution of the aspirate in Jane Austen's Great Britain; mine was to consult the formidable knowledge of my colleague J. A. Miller.